TABLE OF CONTENTS

Early Prevention of and Intervention for Delinquency and Related Problem Behavior

EARLY PREVENTION OF AND INTERVENTION FOR DELINQUENCY AND RELATED PROBLEM BEHAVIOR

Summary

Issues

Strong evidence links early problem behavior to later adolescent delinquency and serious adult criminality. Many children in the United States are lacking fundamental elements essential for human development. These children are legally entitled, but have no access, to safe shelter, adequate food, basic health care, and sufficient preparation to become economically viable adults. The absence of these resources has been linked to abnormal development, economically and socially marginal existence, and persistent criminality.

Children whose parents are criminals have a high probability of becoming delinquents. Those identified in court as abused or neglected by their parents are more likely than other children to become delinquent. Offenders whose parents were also criminals have a high probability of being high-rate predatory criminals. However, whether or not their parents have criminal histories, children raised by mothers or fathers with good parenting skills are less likely to become delinquents or serious offenders. Inmates who assume responsible family roles after they are released are less likely to recidivate than offenders without family ties. The vast majority of delinquents and criminals eventually "mature out" of crime; assumption of family responsibilities can be a key factor in this process.

Research documents the effectiveness of early prevention and intervention in forestalling these outcomes. Waiting until the mid-to-late teenage years to intervene in persistent delinquency ensures that the battle will be difficult, if not impossible. The current focus on older juveniles is at best a stopgap measure; it ignores younger children, who, in the absence of early prevention/intervention, will soon follow the same non-productive path as their teenage role models. Research also suggests that early childhood programs cost relatively little compared to the costs associated with the problems they prevent later, such as drug and alcohol abuse, teen pregnancy, special education requirements, or institutionalization.

Successful early childhood programs when compared to less successful ones most often have these characteristics:

- They attempt to ameliorate more than one or two factors associated with delinquency and focus on multiple problem behaviors.

- They are designed to be appropriate for children of specific ages and at specific stages of development.

- They involve long-term efforts of more than a few months, often lasting several years.

Based on the above and other current research, the task force policy recommendations focus on how the U.S. Department of Justice can assist with early prevention and intervention.

Policy recommendations

- **Early prevention.** The U.S. Department of Justice should take a leading role in the interagency development of early prevention efforts that have shown evidence of being effective, in particular:

  ❑ Establishment of home visitation programs for mothers at high risk for abusing, neglecting, or inadequately providing for the needs of their children.

❏ Establishment of educational daycare programs with a home visitation component for at-risk infants and children that provide assistance to parents, teach parenting skills, and involve marital and family therapy.

❏ De facto, as well as de jure, provision of services to which children and adolescents are legally entitled, especially services essential to their safety and wholesome development (e.g., development of neighborhood-based collaborative community development and youth development programs that emphasize provision of basic needs for infants and preschool children and actively recruit and sustain participation of older children in the nonschool hours).

■ **Criminal parents.** Early prevention and intervention efforts should be targeted to parents who are under supervision of the criminal and juvenile justice systems and the family courts. In the short term, these efforts can reduce crimes committed by parents; in the long term, they can reduce future crimes that might otherwise be committed by the children of offenders and interrupt the cycle of criminal behavior in sequential generations. Promising approaches include:

❏ Prenatal counseling, perinatal care (including substance abuse treatment) for pregnant offenders, and hands-on parenting classes for offenders with babies and young children.

❏ Therapeutic communities or similar residential programs, especially those that help inmates in assessing and improving their interactions with children and spouses, for prison or jail inmates who are within a year of release or who have just been released.

❏ Family focus/parenting programs with active door-to-door outreach in communities in which many children have fathers in jail or prison. Referral and advocacy for health, nutrition, and related services for children of parents under juvenile/criminal justice system supervision or conditional release.

❏ Recruitment of more stable extended family members to care for the children of offenders, especially in cultural groups in which the extended family has traditionally played a key role in childrearing.

■ **Juvenile offenders.** Programs should be developed to assist families of youths 10 to 12 years old who are coming to the attention of the juvenile justice system. For older, more persistent juvenile offenders, community-based programs that focus on behavioral skills should be developed.

■ **Research needs.** The Department of Justice should design and support high-quality evaluations of major prevention and intervention programs, including those described above as promising, for pre- and post-natal children, preschool-age children, school-age children, and school-age youths.

EARLY PREVENTION OF AND INTERVENTION FOR DELINQUENCY AND RELATED PROBLEM BEHAVIOR

Three types of recommendations for policies and actions relevant to the Department of Justice have been generated from a review of current research knowledge about early prevention and intervention. These are recommendations for (1) general prevention strategies best implemented in collaboration with other Federal agencies; (2) prevention/intervention strategies within the justice system; and (3) additional justice system research needs.

General strategies. The ASC Task Force recommends that the U.S. Department of Justice take a leading role in the interagency development of early prevention efforts. Specific recommendations are (1) the establishment of home visitation programs for mothers at high risk for abusing, neglecting, or inadequately providing for the needs of their children; (2) the establishment of educational daycare programs with a home visitation component for at-risk infants and children; and (3) the active assurance of provision to children and adolescents of services to which they are **legally** entitled, especially services essential to their safety and wholesome development.

Strategies within the justice system. The ASC Task Force recommends that the U.S. Department of Justice target early prevention and intervention efforts on parents under supervision of the justice system—including the criminal justice system, juvenile justice system, and family courts. Fostering family skills can reduce crimes committed by the parents, prevent future crimes committed by the children of offenders, and interrupt the cycle of criminal behavior in sequential generations.

The ASC Task Force recommends the development of programs to assist families of younger youths (ages 10 to 12 years) coming to the attention of family courts or the justice system. For older, persistently delinquent youths, we recommend the development and replication of community-based programs with demonstrated effectiveness in promoting productive prosocial behavior and constructive skills, including,

for those who already are parents, family interventions to promote good parenting skills.

Additional justice system research needs. We recommend the design and support of high-quality evaluations of major prevention and intervention programs, including types of programs noted as "promising approaches" in this document.

The following document summarizes the research findings that form the basis for these recommendations and presents the recommendations in more detail.

A Brief Review of the Research and Specific Research-Based Recommendations [1]

Introduction

The critical importance of early prevention and intervention for reducing delinquency, crime, and violence has been consistently documented by research findings. There is clear indication that problem behavior often begins early in life, and there is strong evidence of substantial continuity between problem behavior in early childhood and later adolescent delinquency and serious adult criminality. "An ounce of prevention is worth more than a pound of cure" is more than an old adage. Not only can early prevention and intervention reduce future crime and delinquency, but waiting until the mid-to-late teenage years to intervene in serious, persistent delinquency commonly results in an uphill and all too frequently fruitless battle.

Intervening with youths whose life histories have resulted in entrenched delinquent and violent behavior is difficult and, at best, ends with uncertain results. Also, the current focus on older youths does little about the younger children who will soon follow the same nonproductive paths as the older, seriously delinquent youths in their families and communities.

The current focus on older juveniles is at best a stop-gap measure; in the coming years, in the absence of effective early prevention and intervention, younger delinquents will replace today's older serious delinquents.

While many delinquency/violence prevention programs target high-risk youths in the 13- to 18-year-old age range, many of these programs involve activities with uncertain or unproven outcomes. Common approaches incorporated in current delinquency prevention programs—such as after-school recreation, conflict resolution, mentoring, and employment programs, as well as anti-violence school curriculums—may be desirable for reasons unrelated to delinquency prevention; however, the value of such programs in reducing delinquency and violence remains more a matter of speculation than of empirically demonstrated fact. Rather, it is at the younger ages where promising results have been more fully demonstrated.

As requested by Attorney General Janet Reno in her November 1995 address to the American Society of Criminology, this document briefly summarizes current research understanding about early prevention and intervention approaches that are and are not likely to reduce crime and delinquency. The summary is followed by three types of research-based recommendations: recommendations for (1) general prevention strategies best implemented in collaboration with other Federal agencies; (2) prevention/intervention strategies within the justice system; and (3) additional justice system research needs.

Common Elements and Successful Approaches for Early Prevention and Intervention

Several recent reviews of prevention research and evaluation literature independently concluded that promising results have been achieved by early childhood programs with a set of common characteristics. Compared to less successful programs, successful programs are most often: (1) more comprehensive, attempting to ameliorate more than one or two factors associated with delinquency and simultaneously focusing on multiple problem behaviors; (2) designed to be appropriate for children of specific ages and at specific stages of development; and (3) long-term efforts

of more than a few months, often lasting several years.

Among the most successful primary prevention programs at early ages are home visitation programs that target young, usually single, mothers during their pregnancy and provide assistance for mother and child up to age 2 or 3; enriched preschool (Head Start) programs that incorporate home visitation and provide assistance to parents; or programs that teach parenting skills, assisting parents with troublesome youngsters and involving marital and family therapy. All of these program types have been demonstrated to reduce future crime and violence, as well as related forms of problem behavior, and provide greater assurance of developing a more successful life course for the youngsters involved.

Research has suggested that a sevenfold savings in public expenditures can be achieved by implementing effective early childhood programs; they cost relatively little compared to the costs associated with the problems they prevent in later childhood and the teen years: drug and alcohol abuse, teen pregnancy, special education requirements, and other educational and special needs of delinquents. Similarly, other studies have indicated that early intervention programs that prevent violent crime cost the same as, or less than, institutionalizing older, seriously delinquent youths (and early intervention is much more cost effective when other costs associated with serious delinquency in the teen years are considered). In both the short term and the long run, targeting delinquent adolescents with a "get tough, lock them up" program costs more and is less effective in reducing crime than intervention in early childhood.

Other Promising Approaches Involving School-Age Children

Beyond the preschool years, the programs that hold the greatest promise for preventing delinquency and reducing recidivism among already-delinquent children are those that incorporate multiple approaches for promoting positive behavior and teaching social and other life skills. Programs that are provided in a community setting have had better results than those implemented in an institutional environment. There is also some evidence that promising results may be achieved by strategies and programs that involve: changes in school ecology/organization (especially those that increase parent involvement), monitoring and rewards for good behavior, providing special help from tutors and others for those identified by diagnostic/prescriptive methods, special education programs for disruptive middle- and high-school students, and the currently popular programs for conflict resolution and cognitive behavioral anti-violence curriculums. In general, however, although they appear promising, these programs have not been evaluated with regard to their ability to reduce delinquency, violence, or other problem behaviors.

In addition, some studies have found that after-school recreation programs (both school- and community-based) can reduce delinquent involvement. It must be carefully noted, however, that such programs are only successful if they aggressively recruit youths and work to maintain high participation rates. Simple provision of recreational programs is not sufficient.

Although evaluations of employment/vocational/job-training programs for adults have indicated their effectiveness, similar outcomes for programs aimed at juveniles have not been realized unless a major educational component has been incorporated. Since these findings have been replicated in a number of studies, and since employment and job opportunities for school-age children are popular, stress should be placed on frequently used delinquency-reduction approaches and the need for a significant educational component.

Current Programs for School-Age Youths

Even the best prevention and intervention programs for school-age children have been unable to greatly reduce delinquency, nor should they be expected to significantly reduce the proportion of delinquent youths who will come to the attention of the justice system. Some argue that such programs can be expected to reduce recidivism among already adjudicated adolescents by no more than about 5 percent. While more significant results can be expected from efforts that focus on school-age children who are younger than those who are typically adjudicated—i.e., children who are 10, 11, and 12 years of age—the

juvenile justice system seldom acts in cases involving such youngsters. And in neighborhoods where delinquency rates are high and effective prevention programs are most needed, there is a dearth of community-based organizations with staff trained to promote positive behavior and teach life skills to youths. Too frequently, resources for delinquency prevention are being used for types of programs that have been found consistently to have no effect—including psychotherapy, intensive social casework, employment/vocational programs without an educational component, and peer counseling. Moreover, Federal funds for delinquency prevention are being congressionally earmarked for unproven programs offered by organizations with more political clout than demonstrated success.

Implications

Although it might be considered beyond the direct purview of the U.S. Department of Justice (DOJ), a proactive agency role in the development of early prevention efforts is suggested by the demonstrated positive effects and cost effectiveness of early childhood prevention strategies in reducing future long-term involvement in delinquency (and by inference, later criminality). In particular, DOJ could be the vanguard for interagency efforts promoting the widespread use of home visitation programs for high-risk mothers and educational daycare programs with a home visitation component. The Department can also encourage the implementation of strategies that focus on improving the nurturing skills of parents who are under the supervision of the justice system and who have infants and preschool children. Rather than continuing to fund the implementation of programs known to be ineffective or counterproductive, replications and evaluations of promising programs are strongly suggested.

Through continuing support for studies such as the Project on Human Development in Chicago Neighborhoods (National Institute of Justice) and the Program of Research on the Causes and Correlates of Delinquency (Office of Juvenile Justice and Delinquency Prevention), DOJ has been and continues to be at the forefront of developing basic research information on which to design prevention and intervention programs. However, development of and support for the evaluation of promising programs lags way behind. As a result, there are many promising ongoing and new prevention strategies about which we know practically nothing.

While it is extremely important to continue and to expand basic research efforts, it is also critical to ensure that major prevention and intervention initiatives are adequately evaluated. Without such evaluation, the knowledge on which to base informed decisions about prevention and intervention strategies—including the "get tough" and "increased incarceration" initiatives now in vogue—is simply not available. The likelihood of wasting a great deal of effort and considerable expenditure on ineffective programs that do little to reduce delinquency, crime, and violence is very large.

The absence of adequate evaluation information results in a climate in which unproven popular fads become the interventions of today—and the butt of arguments tomorrow about the futility of prevention. Let us use what we know now about what works to provide more effective prevention—and learn more about what works, so we can do better in the future.

Recommendations for General Strategies

■ **Research-based recommendation:** We recommend that the U.S. Department of Justice take a leading role in the interagency development of early prevention efforts. In particular, we advocate the establishment of (1) home visitation programs for mothers at high risk for abusing, neglecting, or inadequately providing for the needs of their children, and (2) educational daycare programs with a home visitation component for at-risk infants and children.

Summary of research basis for recommendation: Consistent research and evaluation findings indicate that these two kinds of programs can substantially reduce later delinquency and criminality. They also can reduce other individual health and mental health problems and lead to more positive outcomes for the youths involved. It is estimated that early childhood programs such as these can save future public expenditures at a 1:7 ratio. In addition, early prevention programs are at least as, and often more, cost effective than crime reduction approaches that depend on

incapacitation and long-term sentences for older delinquent youths, even when only justice system costs are considered.

■ **Research-based recommendation:** We recommend that decisonmakers pursue de facto as well as de jure provision of services to which children and adolescents are legally entitled, especially services essential to their safety and wholesome development.

Summary of research basis for recommendation: Many children in the United States are lacking fundamental elements essential for human development. While these children are legally entitled to safe shelter, adequate food, basic health care, and sufficient preparation for adult economic viability, the actual lack of access to these resources has been linked to a failure to develop normally, to economically and socially marginal lives, and to persistent criminality.

Promising approaches:

❑ Better accountability and quality assurance in public and private agencies mandated to provide essential resources for infants, toddlers, and school-age children.

❑ Advocates who are able to help caregivers and adolescents circumvent bureaucratic barriers in agencies mandated to provide essential resources.

❑ Neighborhood-based youth-development organizations that provide sustained and comprehensive support and opportunities needed for wholesome development from early childhood through the teen years.

Approach shown by research to be ineffective:

❑ Services provided by traditional social welfare organizations.

Recommendations for Strategies Within the Justice System

Based on consistent research findings on early prevention and intervention, there are several recommendations directly related to the justice system.

Research-based recommendation: Target early prevention and intervention efforts on parents under supervision of the justice system—including the criminal justice system, juvenile justice system, and family courts. In the short term, these can reduce crimes committed by the parents; in the long term, they can reduce future crimes committed by the children of offenders and interrupt the cycle of criminal behavior in sequential generations.

Summary of research basis for recommendation: Children whose parents are criminals have a relatively high probability of becoming delinquents. Children identified in court as having been abused or neglected by their parents are more likely than other children to become delinquent. Offenders whose parents were also criminals have a high probability of being high-rate predatory criminals. However, whether or not their parents have criminal histories, children raised by mothers or fathers with good parenting skills are less likely to become delinquent and serious offenders.

Inmates who assume responsible family roles after they are released are less likely to recidivate than offenders who do not have family ties. The vast majority of delinquents and criminals eventually "mature out of crime"; assumption of family responsibilities can be a key factor in this process.

Promising approaches:

❑ Prenatal counseling, perinatal care for pregnant offenders, and hands-on parenting classes for offenders with babies and young children. Since a majority of women offenders are substance abusers, substance abuse treatment is frequently an important component of perinatal care for offenders.

❑ Therapeutic communities (TC's) or similar residential programs for prison or jail inmates who are within a year of release and who have just been released; in particular, TC's in which inmates receive professional help in assessing and improving their interactions with children and spouses.

❑ Family focus/parenting programs with active door-to-door outreach in communities in which

many children have fathers in jail or prison. Referral and advocacy for health, nutrition, and related services for children of parents under juvenile/criminal justice system supervision or conditional release.

❑ Accessible educational services/employment-skills training for young mothers, especially in tandem with Head Start-type childcare for their infants and toddlers and more traditional Head Start childcare for their preschool-age children.

❑ Recruitment of more stable extended family members to care for the children of offenders—especially in cultural groups in which the extended family has traditionally played a key role in child rearing.

❑ Neighborhood-based collaborative community- and youth-development programs that emphasize provision of basic needs for infants and preschool children and actively recruit and sustain participation of older children during nonschool hours.

Approach shown by research to be counterproductive:

❑ Repeated out-of-extended-family placements of children of offenders (including out-of-extended-family placement for neglected/abused children).

Research-based recommendation: Develop programs to assist families of younger youths (10- to 12-year-olds) coming to the attention of the justice system. For older, persistent offenders, develop behavioral skill-oriented community-based programs.

Summary of research basis of recommendation: Planned services for families of younger youths coming to the attention of the juvenile justice system (police and courts) are minimal, often because the behavior of these youths is not seen as dangerous. Yet youths who become involved in delinquency before they are adolescents are at higher risk for future involvement in crime than youths who become delinquent at later ages. Parents who seek help for such youths most frequently turn to schools. Most schools are not prepared to provide services consistently found to reduce delinquency effectively, such as parent training and home visits to assist in family processes.

Promising approaches:

❏ Referrals of 10-, 11-, and 12-year-olds detained by the police to neighborhood organizations providing sustained activities during the nonschool hours, under the guidance of adults trained to provide the types of support and opportunities young adolescents and their families benefit from and enjoy.

❏ Provision of support services to the families of such youths, in particular, parent training and home visitation programs to assist in family organization, social skills, and problem solving.

❏ For older teens who have persistently been engaging in delinquent behavior, placement in communal detention settings where youths gradually earn status and privileges through vocational achievement and through contributions to the welfare of all in the "community"— followed by supervised participation in similar activities after they earn their way out of detention.

Approaches shown by research to be ineffective or counterproductive:

❏ Secure detention for adolescents.

❏ Any form of detention in the absence of transitional care on return to the community.

❏ Programs consisting of short-term efforts to fix individual deficits or to prevent a particular type of delinquent behavior.

❏ Employment/job programs for school-age youths (despite their success for adults) that do NOT include a major educational component.

❏ Programs implemented by organizations that are experiencing fiscal or administrative difficulties. Also, programs implemented by organizations with little or no proven experience in delinquency prevention and youth development but, because of political connections, receive Federal "pork-barrel" funding.

Recommendations for Meeting Additional Justice System Research Needs

Research-based recommendation: Design and support high-quality evaluations of major prevention and intervention programs, including types of programs noted as "promising approaches" in this document.

Summary of research basis for recommendation: Almost all reviews of early prevention and intervention programs observe that there is a dearth of valid evaluation information about a wide variety of promising programs. The Office of Justice Programs has been a leader and continues to be at the forefront of developing basic research information on which to design prevention and intervention programs, including much of the research conducted by ASC members that forms the basis of this report.

However, development of and support for the evaluation of promising programs lags way behind. While evaluation findings form the basis for programs and approaches described in this paper as promising, most evaluations have been limited to studying the implementation process or outcomes in a few sites. Without systematic replication and evaluation, we cannot at this time definitively recommend national implementation of some of the most promising programs and approaches described here. In addition, there are many other potentially promising ongoing and newly developed prevention strategies about which we know practically nothing.

It is critical to ensure that major prevention and intervention initiatives are adequately evaluated. Without such evaluation, information about ongoing programs, including the "get tough" and "increased incarceration" initiatives now in vogue, solid findings that can form the basis for decisions about prevention and intervention strategies are simply not available. Without adequate evaluation, the likelihood is great that a great deal of effort and considerable expenditure will be wasted on ineffective programs that do little to reduce delinquency, crime, or violence.

Note

1. Recommendations are based on research reported in over 100 publications authored by members of the American Society of Criminology (ASC). Given the purpose of this document to briefly summarize this literature and draw on consistent findings for policy and practice, it does not reference the individual findings of the many researchers who contributed to our current understanding of early prevention and intervention for delinquency and related problems. However, several ASC members conducted their own reviews of an extensive corpus of research that are incorporated in this document, and we would like to acknowledge their efforts; they are Richard Catalano, David Farrington, Peter Greenwood, Nancy Guerra, J. David Hawkins, Adele Harrell, Mark Lipsey, Patrick Tolan, and Franklin Zimring.

Youth
Violence

YOUTH VIOLENCE

Issues

Sharp increases in juvenile violence have heightened the sense of personal risk experienced by those who live and work in urban areas and contributed strongly to the widespread fear of crime in general. This fear derives from the randomness (the perpetrators and victims of juvenile homicides are strangers about 30 percent of the time), early onset, and seriousness of violence perpetrated by youths. Between 1985 and 1992, the juvenile homicide arrest rate, the juvenile homicide victimization rate, the number of juvenile homicides involving guns, and the rates of murder committed by 15- and 16-year olds increased by more than 100 percent. In addition, the arrest rate of nonwhite juveniles for drug offenses doubled. Public anxiety extends beyond fears for personal safety to include concerns about an irreparable breach of the social contract.

A working hypothesis about the growth in juvenile violence is as follows:

- When crack cocaine hit the streets in 1985, it changed illegal drug buying habits and distribution patterns. The number of transactions increased markedly, as people bought one "hit" at a time, rather than larger quantities that could be stored for later use.

- To accommodate the higher number of transactions, youths (primarily African Americans in center-city areas) were recruited into the drug market.

- Since they could not easily ask the police for protection, the new recruits needed guns to protect themselves and their valuable wares.

- Their tight networking through schools and the streets led to a broader diffusion of guns into the larger youthful community, primarily for self-defense but also, perhaps, for status.

Summary

- Because of the presence of guns, the fights that routinely occur among youths can rapidly turn from fist fights to shootings. Adult gun carriers, even those in the drug market, seem better able to exercise restraint.

- As more young people carried guns, they provided an incentive for other youths to arm themselves, resulting in an escalating process of gun-carrying (the familiar "arms race"), which, in turn, has led to a greater propensity in any dispute for either party to use his gun before the other person does.

The key here is the "diffusion hypothesis," which suggests that the growth in juvenile homicides is a consequence of adoption within the larger community of behavior endemic to the drug industry: carrying guns and using them to settle disputes. The diffusion hypothesis is supported by the fact that, since 1985, the homicide arrest rates of both white and nonwhite juveniles have grown, respectively, by 80 percent and 120 percent, although there has been no evident growth in the involvement of white youths in the drug market.

Policy recommendations

- **Guns on the street.** Because carrying a handgun is illegal almost everywhere, the task of getting guns out of the hands of juveniles requires stronger and more focused enforcement of existing legislation. The Federal Government's main role should be to offer technical assistance to localities that would like to pursue this strategy but need help in doing so. For example, the recent National Institute of Justice (NIJ) project in Kansas City came out with some important findings with regard to approaches for capturing illegal guns. Even if we were to stop the flow of guns to and from drug markets, we still have to worrry about the guns that are already present in the streets.

■ **Guns in the market.** Illicit gun markets (especially those that sell to kids, and especially in urban areas) must be more tightly controlled. Law enforcement has focused on the drug market while largely ignoring the market for illegal firearms. The challenge is a clear Federal responsibility because so much of the traffic in guns is interstate.

■ **Treatment and prevention.** Consideration should be given to shrinking the size of drug markets by siphoning off some of the demand for drugs. Measures should include increasing the resources and effort put into treatment and prevention and finding ways to bring certified addicts into treatment programs, like those who are being supported under the SSI program.

■ **Socialization of youth.** In the long run, we must face the widespread problem of socializing the growing number of young people who see no hope for their economic future and are willing, therefore, to take whatever risks are necessary to gain respect and earn an income. These disenfranchised youths represent ready recruits for any illicit markets that present themselves.

YOUTH VIOLENCE

Background and Public Concerns

One of the important sources of widespread public fear of crime is the enhanced sense of risk resulting from the increase in juvenile violence. This fear has led policymakers to resort to draconian legislative responses (such as broad-scope three-strikes laws) focused on sweeping increases in the use of incarceration to control crime that are not likely to be effective and are likely to represent a major burden on criminal justice systems and taxpayers.

Thus it is important that we examine the facts that reflect changes that have taken place during the past decade involving juveniles in violence, with particular emphasis on the aspect of violence that is probably most fear-inducing—juvenile homicide. The fear derives partly from a variety of considerations that create a sense of randomness when juveniles act violently. Juvenile homicides involve strangers about 50 percent more often than do adult homicides: about 30 percent of juvenile homicides are random compared with about 20 percent of adult homicides.

These concerns are exacerbated by the presence of guns—especially assault weapons with high firepower—as a major factor in juvenile homicides. In light of doubts about their marksmanship and grave concern about their using weapons at the slightest provocation, many people who might otherwise feel safe from homicide are very troubled at the prospect of being engulfed by the sense of escalating juvenile violence. The fear also undoubtedly involves some concern that goes beyond personal risk and must raise some anxiety about the unraveling of the social fabric as we learn about growing rates of misdeeds by the "upcoming generation."

Some Facts About Juvenile Violence

In contrast to burglary and robbery, which are crimes that peak sharply in the late teens and early twenties, the age distribution of murder arrestees has traditionally been quite flat. Until 1985, the peak of the age-specific arrest rate (the "age-crime curve") for murder had a flat rate, which hovered around the same value (about 25 per 100,000) for all the ages of 18 through 24 for the entire period 1970 through 1985. During this period, the rates for the ages under 18 were also quite low; for 16-year-olds, for example, the rate had been an almost constant rate of 12 per 100,000 from 1970 through 1985.

This picture of considerable stability in most things related to homicide changed rather dramatically beginning in about 1985, as crack entered the national consciousness. The change in 1985 was a change from fairly stable, constant trends, to a sudden upward change in direction, although the transition point was different in different places. There is a widespread sense that there is a drug connection in all this, although most people would guess that the connection is pharmacological—young people get high on drugs, which makes them lose their inhibitions, and that gives rise to all the killing.

Between 1985 and 1992, we suddenly saw an upward growth in the rate of homicides by young people, their use of guns in homicides, and very sharp growth in the involvement of nonwhite juveniles in the drug industry. All of these factors had been quite stable for nearly 15 years, leading in just 7 years to the following major changes:

- More than doubling of the juvenile homicide arrest rate (with no change in the rates for adults over the age of 24). See figures 1a and 1b.

- More than doubling of the juvenile homicide victimization rate (with no comparable growth in the adult victimization rate). See figure 2.

- More than doubling of the number of juvenile homicides involving the use of guns (with no change in the number of nongun homicides). See figure 3.

- Doubling in the arrest rate of nonwhite juveniles for drug offenses (with no increase in the arrest rate of white juveniles). See figure 4.

Figure 1a: Trends in Age-Specific Murder Rate
Trends for Individual Peak Ages

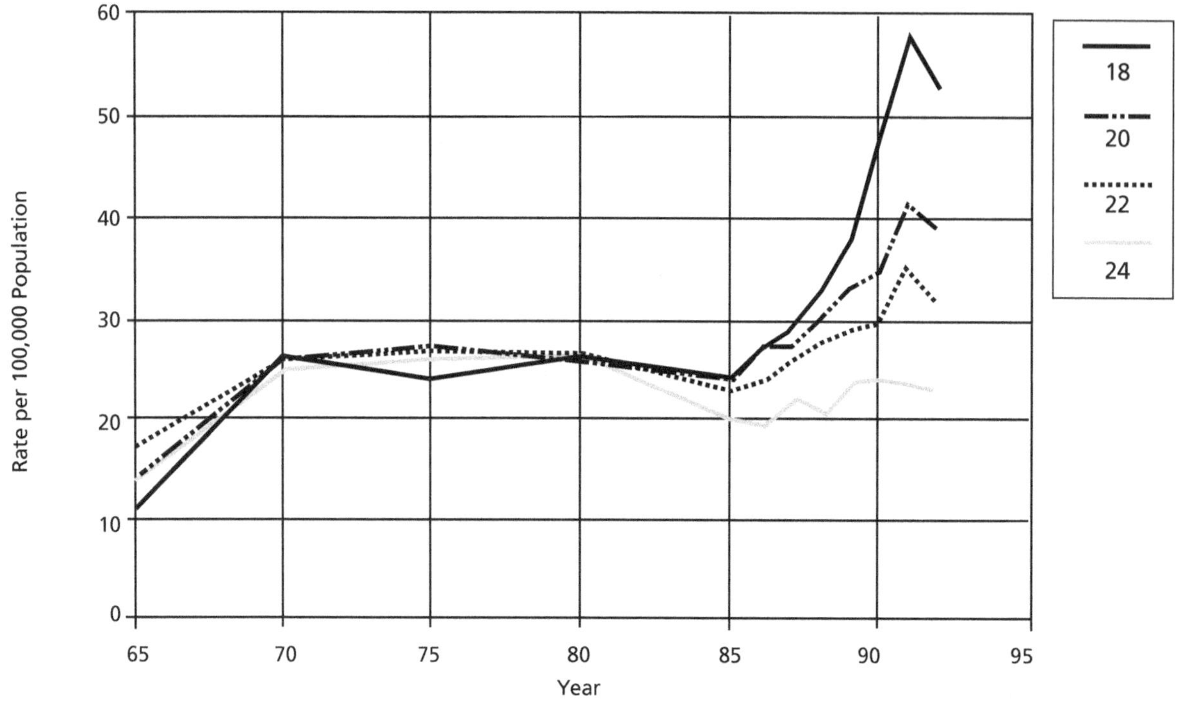

Figure 1b: Trends in Age-Specific Murder Rate
Trends for Individual Young Ages

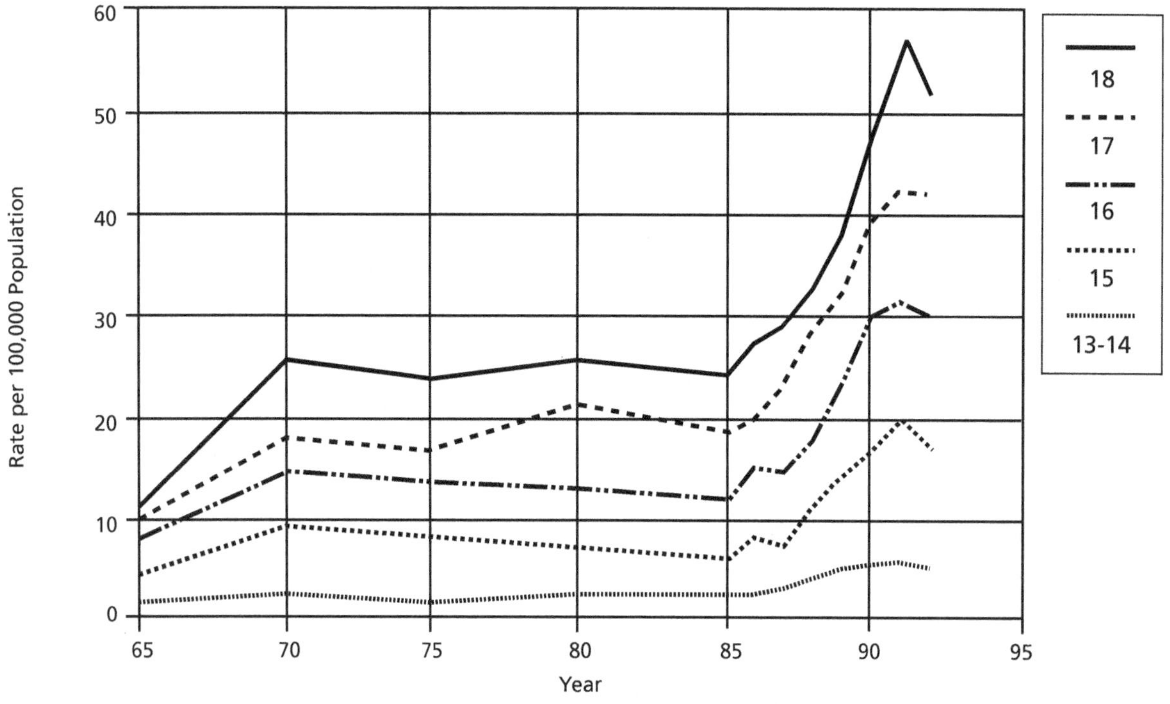

Figure 2: Homicide Rates by Victim Age, 1980–91
White and Black Males, 15–19 and 20–24

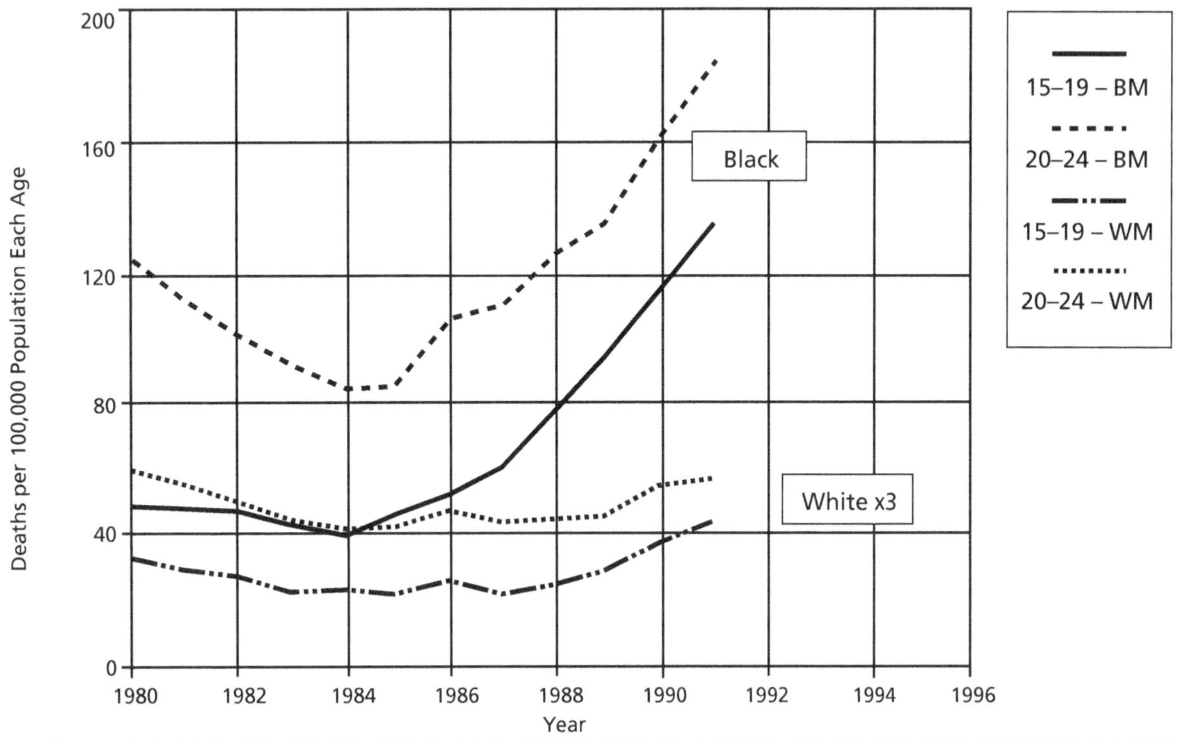

Legend:
- 15–19 – BM
- 20–24 – BM
- 15–19 – WM
- 20–24 – WM

(y-axis: Deaths per 100,000 Population Each Age; x-axis: Year)

Figure 3: Number of Gun and Nongun Homicides
Juvenile Offenders (10–17)

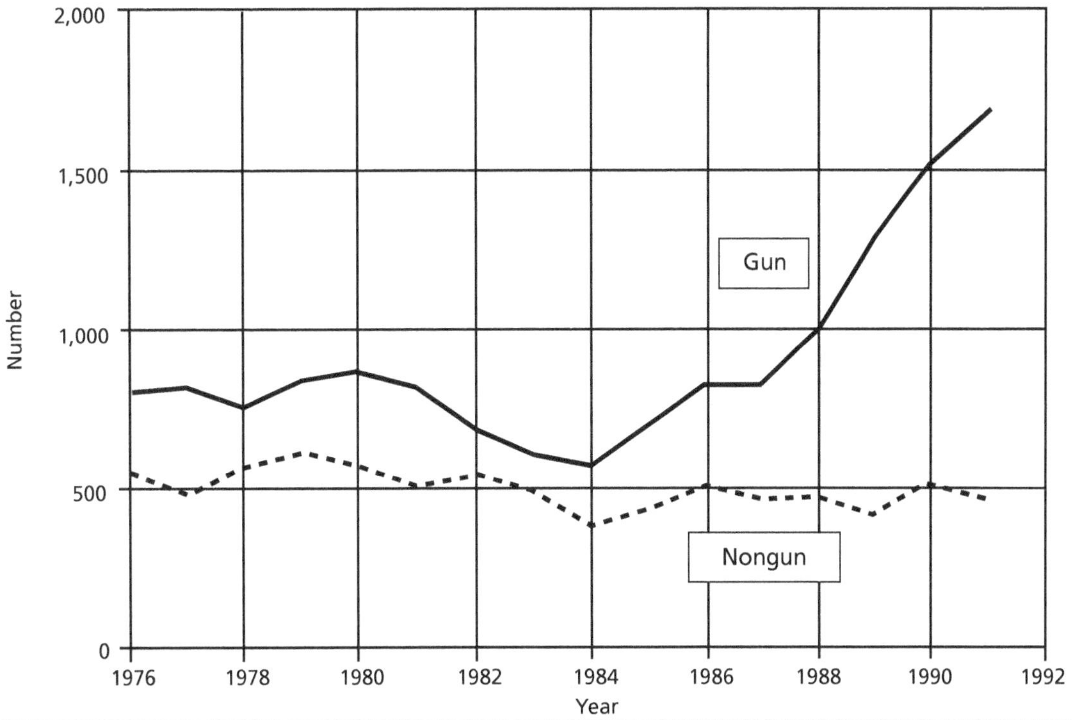

(y-axis: Number; x-axis: Year)

8251

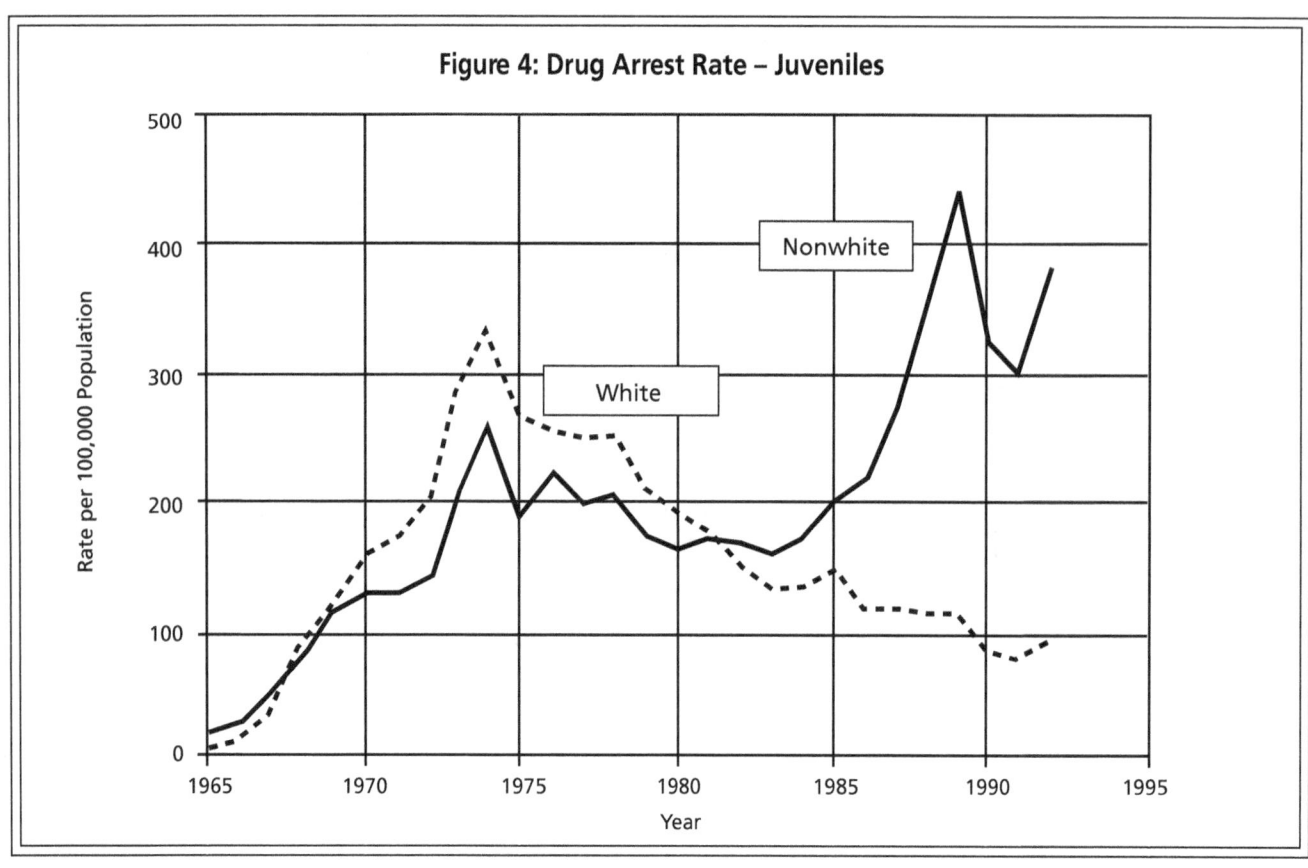

Figure 4: Drug Arrest Rate – Juveniles

The immediate challenge is to figure out what scenario could be connecting these three sharp and sharply focused changes. There is no question that a variety of criminogenic factors in the environment has contributed (or could have contributed) to a worsening crime situation. But it is not easy to identify what changes have occurred that could account for so dramatic a change. For this explanation, we turn to a working hypothesis about the process that seems to have led to the major growth in juvenile violence:

■ With the arrival of crack markets beginning in about 1985, the number of drug transactions increased markedly partly because people were buying a "hit" at a time, rather than buying larger quantities and keeping the inventory in their relatively secure homes.

■ To accommodate this growth in demand for transactions, youths, primarily African Americans in central-city areas, were recruited into those drug markets.

■ Because drug traffickers cannot easily call police for protection, their standard practice is to carry a gun in the drug markets to protect themselves and their valuable wares.

■ The tight networking of youths through schools and the streets has led to a broader diffusion of guns into the larger youthful community, primarily for self-defense but also perhaps for status-seeking. Because adults are less tightly networked, we do not see comparable diffusion among them.

■ As a result of the presence of guns, the fights that are routine among youths can readily turn into shooting rather than merely fist fights. Adults, even though they may also be carrying guns (and particularly those who work in the drug markets), seem much better able to exercise restraint in using guns.

■ The growing presence of guns among youths provides an increased incentive for each additional youth to carry his own gun. This results in an escalating process of gun-carrying (the familiar "arms race"), thereby leading in any dispute to a greater propensity to use the weapon before the other person does.

The key here is the "diffusion hypothesis," which suggests that the growth in the number of homicides by youths attributable to the drug industry is a consequence, not so much of the "systemic" murder within the drug industry (the growth rate seems much too high to be explained only by the limited rates of homicide within the industry), but rather of the adoption within the larger community that is networked with the drug industry of some of the mores that operate within that industry. And prominent among those mores is the carrying of guns and use of them for settling disputes.

The diffusion hypothesis is supported by the fact that since 1985, the growth in the homicide arrest rate of juveniles who are white has grown by 80 percent, and for nonwhite juveniles, it has grown by 120 percent. (See figures 5a and 5b for a comparison of adult and juvenile murder arrest rates over the year.) This growth in the rate of white juveniles arrested for homicide has occurred with no evident growth in involvement in the drug markets by white juveniles. (See figure 4.)

Some Policy Responses

These observations suggest some policy actions, both immediate and longer term, that should be pursued:

■ For the immediate future, we have got to focus on ways to get guns out of the hands of youths, especially in urban areas. Because carrying handguns is illegal almost everywhere, this usually requires stronger and more focused enforcement of existing legislation rather than any new legislation. An important Federal role here is one of technical assistance to localities who would like to pursue this strategy, but need help in doing so. For example, the recent National Institute of Justice project in Kansas City came out with some important results on approaches to capturing illegal guns. Even if we were to stop the flow of guns from the drug markets, we still have to worry about the guns that are already present in the streets.

■ On a somewhat broader basis, we must find means for exercising tighter control over illicit gun markets, especially those that sell guns to youths in

urban areas. There are some interesting parallels here to the illicit drug markets: both peddle dangerous products, and we have been obsessed with one and have largely ignored the other. This challenge is clearly a Federal responsibility because so much trafficking in guns is interstate.

■ Because of the salient role of drug markets as a primary causal factor, and in light of the demonstrated difficulty of impacting those markets with enforcement, this may be the time for considering alternative means of shrinking their size by weakening the demand from those markets. This could include increasing the amount of resources and the effort put into treatment and prevention. It also calls for finding ways to bring into treatment programs certified addicts like those who are being supported under the SSI program, for example.

■ For the longer run, we must face the widespread problem of socializing the growing number of young people who see no hope for their economic future, are willing to take whatever risks are necessary to gain respect and to earn an income, and represent ready recruits for any illicit markets that present themselves.

These suggestions encompass a considerable range of activity, from the immediate police-level activity of confiscating illegal guns in the street to the much broader societal problem of helping to socialize young people whose family—too often a single mother with inadequate education, insufficient employment skills, and little or no external support—lacks the competence or structure to do so effectively.

These suggestions represent important challenges to the Nation. Undoubtedly, each alternative will find strong opposition for reasons that will seem legitimate. Failing to meet these challenges, however, makes it seem that the epidemic of guns and homicide—which has been an important source of distress and fear to the Nation—is likely to continue. And, distress and fear have elicited responses that are likely to ignore the central problem and generally make matters worse for the Nation.

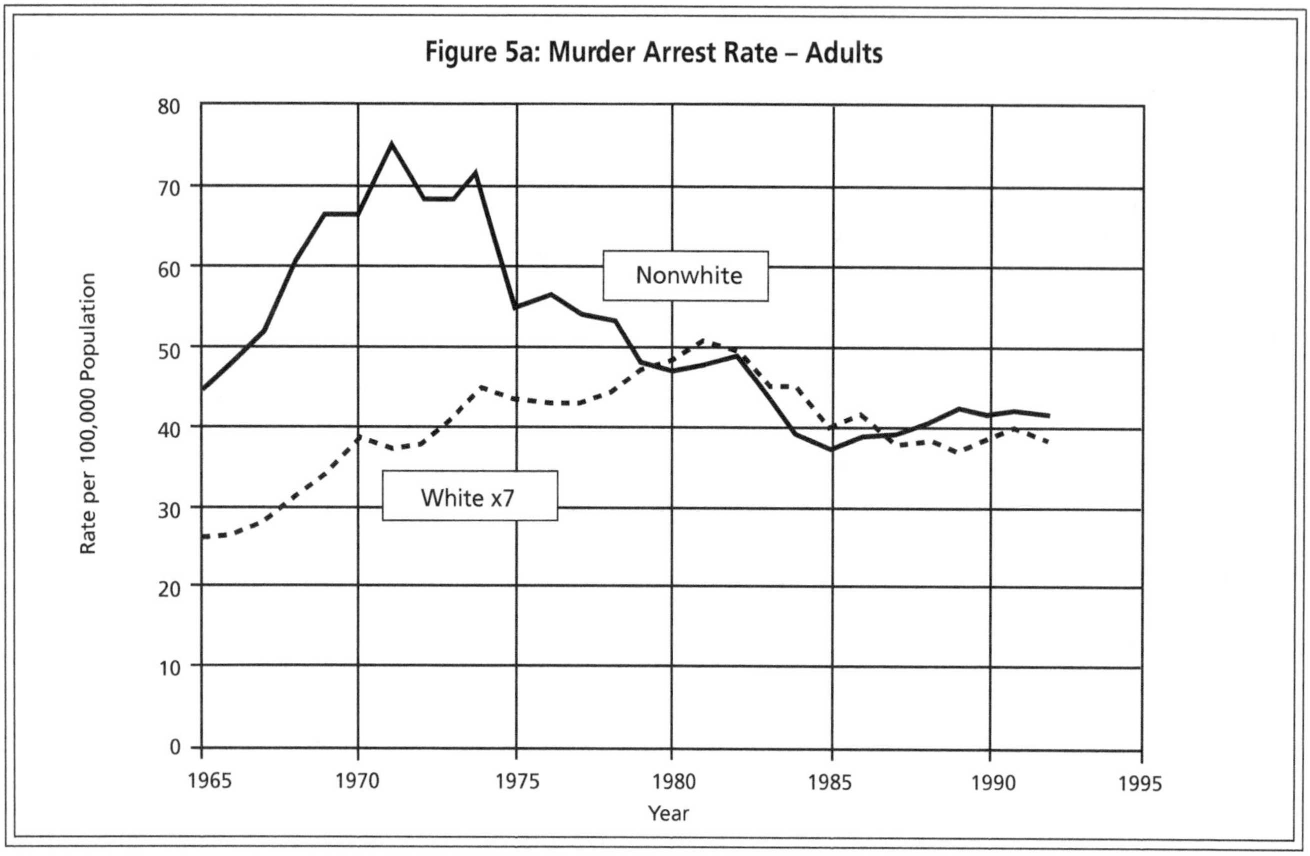
Figure 5a: Murder Arrest Rate – Adults
Rate per 100,000 Population
80
70
60
50
40
30
20
10
0
1965
1970
1975
1980
1985
1990
1995
Year
Nonwhite
White x7

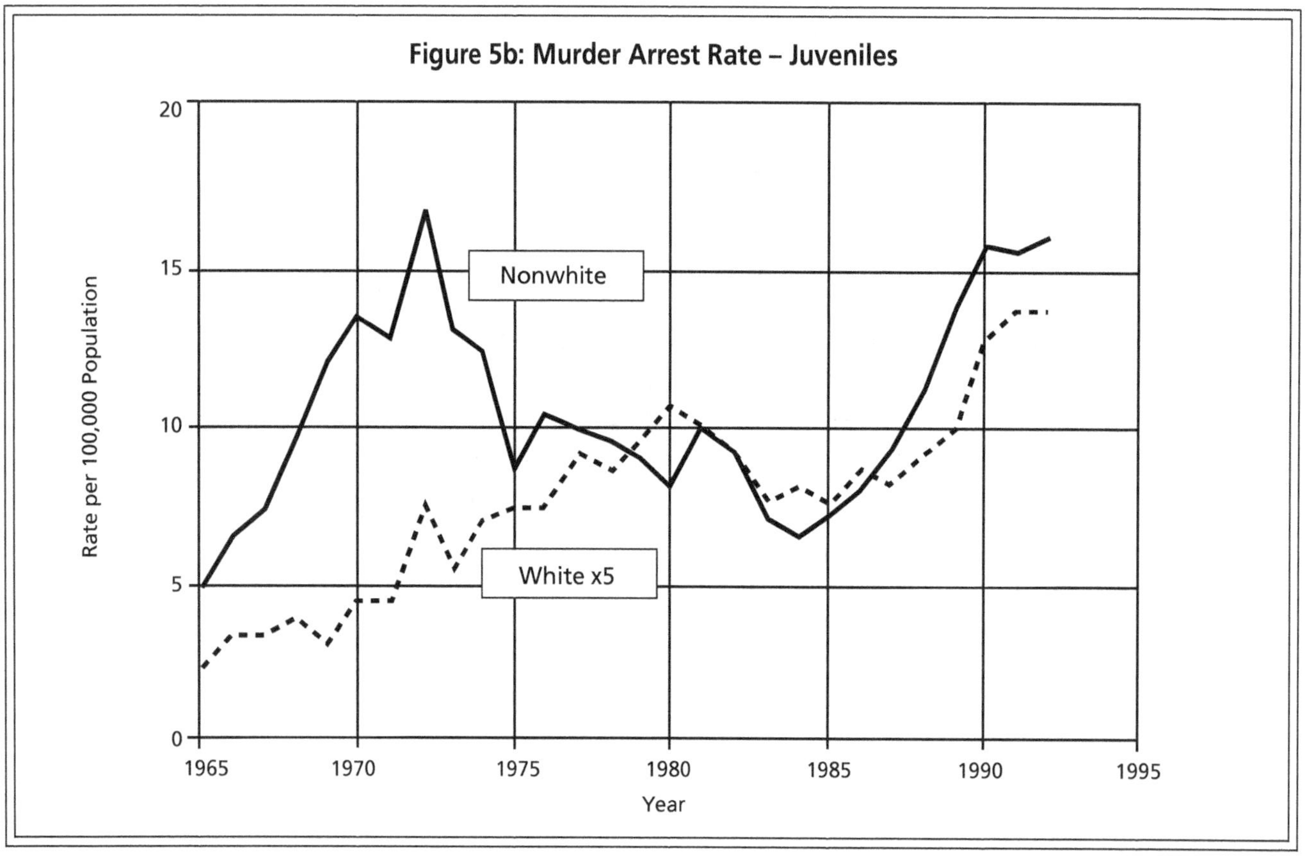
Figure 5b: Murder Arrest Rate – Juveniles
Rate per 100,000 Population
20
15
10
5
0
1965
1970
1975
1980
1985
1990
1995
Year
Nonwhite
White x5

A New Vision for Inner-City Schools

A New Vision for Inner-City Schools

Summary

Issues

Juvenile violence is at an all-time high, and many have decided that only more deterrence measures can effectively deal with delinquency. Criminologists agree that deterrence works well for the average working person with a family and a role in the community. But for people who are unsocialized, impulsive, and mindlessly destructive, deterrence is an ineffective tool. If deterrence is to work, people must be more deterrable.

Adequacy of parenting. Of all the factors found to contribute to delinquency, the clearest and most exhaustive evidence concerns the adequacy of parenting. Abusive, incompetent, or rejecting parents, and those who do not provide sufficient supervision have a direct effect on the antisocial behavior of their children. Poor parenting cannot be viewed as the sole cause of delinquency. The association between inadequate parenting and other factors is, however, critical in predicting future delinquency. These risk factors are parental criminality and drug abuse, prenatal deficiency, lack of education, poor supervision, and deficient discipline. Chief among the factors indicative of later serious delinquency is the age at onset of significant misbehavior. The earlier a child commits a youthful offense, the more likely it is that such delinquency will continue and worsen over time. Therefore, intervention must take place at the earliest possible opportunity if it is to have any lasting effect.

Delinquency and education. Criminologists believe that the problem of delinquency is essentially a problem of socialization. When the family fails in this essential function, the task of socialization must be taken up by the educational system. The criminal justice system can only "pick up the pieces" after delinquency has become a fact.

Inner-city education must be expanded, redesigned, and enriched in order to create a new generation of young people for whom the goal of deterrence has a realistic chance of working.

Policy recommendations

- **Early child-parent intervention.** Both public and private early intervention (birth to age 5) programs should be implemented immediately and include voluntary enrollment, extensive parent training, and frequent home visits; they should be long term, have low student-to-teacher ratios, provide liberal subsidies for working parents, and be competently monitored and evaluated.

- **Early childhood education.** Private early childhood intervention programs that address the needs of the child and the parent should be expanded and subsidized. The Head Start program should be improved by adding parent training and home visits and by extending its term beyond 1 year, especially in areas having a disproportionate number of children at high risk for future delinquency.

- **Pilot residential schools and foster parenting for abused children.** Significant grants should be made for pilot programs to develop a mixture of public and private residential schools, as well as pilot projects for increased funding for foster parenting for children of abusive or demonstrably incompetent parents. When evidence of abuse or neglect is established, when there is a refusal to enter into an existing program of early childhood intervention, and when parental rights have been terminated by court order, we must have placement alternatives readily at hand to raise the affected children in a proper manner.

Residential schools have the potential of being either a blessing or a curse on the minority community. Rather than engaging in politicized debate on the issue of "orphanages," we advocate establishing a number of pilot programs for residential schools that contain the following elements: sufficient funding to ensure an education equal to the residential education available to wealthier families, education that begins at the pre-K level, minority staffing and an emphasis on minority values, and provision for voluntary enrollment.

■ **Pilot community schools.** Well-developed and broad pilot programs should be implemented for development of comprehensive community schools that are run on a districtwide basis (to avoid the problem of stigmatizing children selected as the most at risk). Schooling must go beyond the acquisition of cognitive skills and serve as the focus of many childcare programs, such as prenatal screening, assessment and referral for treatment of developmental problems, and preschool programs that focus on both the child and its parents. These community schools should remain open at night, on weekends, and throughout the year.

■ **Value of properly conducted evaluations.** After evaluating pilot prevention and treatment programs, a limited number of well-funded major interventions with sufficient provision for adequate research design and long-term evaluation should be implemented.

■ **Coordination of educational and criminal justice objectives.** The Department of Justice should coordinate with the Department of Education at the highest level to ensure that the concerns of the law enforcement community are reflected in school curriculums and that the concept of early childhood intervention is accepted as part of a nationwide basic educational policy.

■ **Immediate need to focus on law enforcement alternatives.** Since even the best prevention programs need considerable time to bear fruit, we have no choice but to immediately upgrade our law enforcement alternatives. Knowing full well the ultimate futility of law enforcement for a generation of children who lack elementary socialization and self-control, we are nonetheless obligated to detect and punish those who make life intolerable for others.

A New Vision for Inner-City Schools

Our country is beset by juvenile violence as never before[1] and the electorate is impatient for solutions. Given the generally disappointing results of rehabilitation programs as a whole,[2] many people—and many political leaders—have decided that only more deterrence measures can effectively deal with delinquency and that preventive measures are only so much pork.

Criminologists are in agreement that deterrence does work—but not for everyone. Deterrence works well for the average working person with a family and a role in the community. But for people who are unsocialized, impulsive, and mindlessly self-destructive, deterrence is an ineffective tool. Criminologists have found that for deterrence to work, we need to create not simply more or harsher deterrence measures but more deterrable people. Can this be done? The answer is encouraging: during the last 20 years, criminologists have obtained clear and well-documented data on the key factors involved in delinquency—and have also obtained good evidence to support the view that certain measures actually work in reducing the rate of delinquency and crime.[3] Central to all these programs is the notion of an expanded role for public education.

Background: Delinquency and Parental Adequacy

Of all the factors we have found that contribute to delinquency,[4] the clearest and most exhaustive evidence concerns the adequacy of parenting.[5] Parents who are incompetent, abusive, or rejecting,[6] parents who fail to maintain adequate supervision over their children, and parents who indeed are little more than children themselves have direct effects on the antisocial behavior of their children.[7] Inadequacy of parenting cannot be viewed in isolation as the sole cause of delinquency. However, its association with other factors is critical to predicting future delinquency.[8]

In conjunction with our efforts to identify the most significant risk factors for delinquency (criminality and drug abuse of parents, prenatal deficiency, lack of education, poor supervision, and inadequate disciplinary measures),[9] we have begun to construct and evaluate programs that attempt to counteract these factors.

Chief among the factors indicative of later serious delinquency is the age at onset of significant misbehavior: the earlier the child is found to have committed a youthful offense, the more likely it will be that such delinquency will continue and worsen over time.[10] This finding provides a focus for any discussion of prevention. Intervention must be performed at the earliest possible opportunity if it is to have any lasting effect. Indeed, some criminologists have explained the failure of many programs directed toward adolescent rehabilitation by noting that by the age of adolescence interventions have come too late to be effective.[11] There is widespread agreement among child development professionals that by far the most critical years for social development are birth to age 6.[12] Because of the centrality of parenting as a factor contributing to delinquency and the critical importance of early manifestation of misconduct in predicting future criminality, leading criminologists have looked to early childhood intervention as the most promising societal response to delinquency thus devised.[13]

Delinquency Control and Education Reform

Our system of public education is largely the product of 19th century social reform. It has worked reasonably well for more than a hundred years because it has rested on a well-established assumption: while public education would serve the needs of young people for a limited portion of the day and calendar year, the child's family would adequately provide for the child's development at all other times. Although this may have been a fair assumption for most of America throughout its history, it is certainly not so today. In fact, in our inner cities, the education process breaks down precisely when the school day ends. Children who return to a neighborhood rife with crime and drug abuse, who return to a household with inadequate or nonexistent parenting, are virtually programmed for educational and societal failure despite the best efforts of our school system. For public education to fulfill its mandate—not just to get kids "through school"—to produce responsible, self-sufficient adults, it must provide the means to educate every child, not only those with intact, nurturing families, but also those who are deprived of such life supports. To the extent that a child suffers from such deprivation, the educational system must act as effective parental supplements and substitutes.

We in the field of criminology believe that the problem of delinquency is essentially a problem of socialization. Certainly, the most appropriate and effective means of socialization is the family. But when the family fails in this essential function, the task of socialization must be taken up by the educational system. The criminal justice system, with all its resources to detect, prosecute, and sanction offenders, simply cannot solve the problem of delinquency—it can only pick up the pieces. It is therefore necessary that criminal justice objectives be explicitly recognized by educational policymakers. What we propose in this report is a number of concrete ways in which education in the inner cities can be expanded, redesigned, and enriched to create a new generation of young people for whom the goal of deterrence has a realistic chance of working.

Element One: Expanding Preschool Education

An increasing number of well-documented early childhood intervention programs have demonstrated a significant effect on socialization and delinquency.[14] These programs typically involve:

■ Identification of the at-risk population (i.e., low income, single parenthood, low educational attainment).

■ Early intervention (typically pre-K to first grade).

■ Extensive parent training.

■ Frequent home visits.

■ Duration of several years.

Of the number of such programs instituted in this country, four have been evaluated with adequate research models and over a long enough followup period to track the results into adolescence and early adulthood. These projects are located in Michigan (The Perry School),[15] Houston (Parent-Child Development Center),[16] Syracuse (Child Development Project),[17] and New Haven (Yale Child Welfare Project).[18] Each has shown a lasting reduction in antisocial behavior, delinquency, and adult criminality.[19] Perhaps because these programs are voluntary and are directed strictly toward educational achievement (as opposed to being regarded as delinquency prevention programs), there is no reported evidence of a stigmatizing effect that might interfere with social development.

It is important to stress that these programs were designed to address both the child (cognitive and social development) and the parent (acquisition and monitoring of parental skills). What distinguishes these successful programs from a rash of unsuccessful programs is their multiple components. The causes of criminality and delinquency have been found to be multiple: the more risk factors present, the greater the risk of delinquency. Therefore, the more factors addressed in an intervention plan, the greater the likelihood of success. Neither parent training nor educational supplements alone are sufficient.[20]

Therefore, we recommend an expansion and subsidization of private programs for early childhood intervention that address both the needs of the child and the parent. We further believe that the existing Head Start program can be significantly improved for those who qualify by including parent training, home visits, and a lengthening of its term beyond 1 year.[21]

Element Two: The Community School—a New Vision

For many years, schools have been regarded by social scientists as natural settings for the training of socialization skills.[22] However, programs designed to reduce misconduct have proven to be of little value over extended time periods either because resources have been inadequate or because out-of-school conditions have undermined what is learned in the classroom.[23]

In keeping with our finding that early intervention and multicomponent approaches are the only proven programmatic means of curtailing delinquency for at-risk children, we propose a new concept of public education in the inner cities. We share the vision of Dr. Edward Zigler, one of the founders of Head Start, who proposed that schooling go beyond the acquisition of cognitive skills, which serves as the focus of many childcare programs, such as prenatal screening, assessment and referral for treatment of developmental problems, and preschool programs that focus on both the child and the parent.[24] Just such a concept has been put into effect by Dr. Edward Zigler's "School of the 21st Century," a program that has been adopted in more than 250 communities nationwide.[25] Furthermore, community schools should remain open for these and other activities at night, on weekends, and throughout the year. The justification for 3-month summer vacations has long past: We must not abandon inner-city youths to the streets during these months with the absurd hope that they are somehow going to find jobs.

Element Three: Residential Schools for the Most in Need

It is in the context of redefining the mandate and scope of public education that residential schools become a promising option for children who are fundamentally deprived of effective parenting. For these children, a well-funded, well-equipped, and well-staffed residential school may be their only lifeline to a normal, healthy life.

Despite our efforts at early intervention, we must recognize that increased support services are futile for a significant number of children who are subject to chronic abuse and neglect.[26] Because of the value of family preservation, there is no doubt that outside placement should be used as a last resort only, but when evidence of abuse or neglect is established and when there is a refusal to enter into an existing program of early childhood intervention, we must have parent placement alternatives readily at hand to raise the affected children in a proper manner. Despite the impressive performance of parent training programs, we must consider the large number of

cases where parents are incapable of cooperating.[27] For the parents of such children, out-of-home placement becomes a necessity, either in foster care or a group residence.

We believe that the proposal for the implementation of residential boarding schools for children who are deprived of minimally adequate parenting is a serious one. There has never been a better opportunity for educational reformers of all political persuasions to combine their visions and expertise for the establishment of the kind of residential schools in which we can take pride.

At present, there is much uncertainty as to the long-term effectiveness of residential placement.[28] In addition, the potential cost of residential placement is quite variable[29] and dependent on the extent of physical improvements envisioned, student-teacher ratios, and the amount and quality of services offered. Criminologists and social planners agree, however, that underfunding of residential projects will result in overcrowding, inadequate facilities and services, and in turn, stigmatization of the programs and the students, and educational and social failure. A well-funded program, one that creates beautiful, campus-like environments, with small classes, excellent services, and highly skilled and motivated staff can be instrumental in enabling thousands of children to succeed educationally and socially.

Clearly, there is much at stake in "getting it right." Residential schools have the potential of being either a blessing or a curse on the minority community. Therefore, rather than engaging in politicized debates on the issue of "orphanages," we advocate the establishment of a number of pilot programs for residential schools that have the best chance of succeeding. These should contain the following elements:

■ Funding sufficient to ensure an education for the children that equals residential education available to wealthier families.

■ Schooling that begins at the pre-K level.

■ Minority staffing and emphasis on respect for minority cultural values.

■ Provision for voluntary enrollment.

Also, rather than advocating a policy of one or more placement alternatives, we recommend the establishment of significant grants for the development of a mixture of public and private residential schools for children of abusive or demonstrably incompetent parents and pilot projects for increased funding for foster parenting. The results of these pilot projects will be critical to the development of social policies that can be applied on a large-scale basis during the next century.

Timetable for Implementation

Despite our impatience for solutions and despite our enthusiasm for innovative programs, we must acknowledge that, on the whole, government programs designed to combat delinquency have been disappointing.[30] Therefore, we must approach larger scale implementation with great care. We have learned that, in terms of long-term effects on delinquency, half a loaf is not better than none.[31] Piecemeal solutions are not only unproductive and wasteful but tend to diminish the chances for effective measures by discouraging people against prevention generally. The time schedule for implementation should be dependent on the degree of proven success of each of the projects mentioned. Therefore, we propose a project implementation program as follows:

Immediate implementation of early intervention programs. The success of early child-parent intervention programs is documented well enough at this point to suggest national implementation and replication with both private and public options. In this replication process we must insist that these programs include the following key factors:

■ Voluntary enrollment.

■ Early intervention (birth to age 5).

■ Extensive parent training.

■ Frequent home visitation.

■ Duration of several years.

■ Low student-teacher ratios.

■ Liberal subsidies for working parents.

■ Competent monitoring and evaluation.

As an alternative to subsidized, private-sector programs of child care, we also recommend that the existing Head Start program be upgraded to consist of the above features, at least in those geographical areas having a high proportion of children most at risk for future delinquency.

Establishment of pilot programs for expanded community schools and residential schools. These programs and proposals, unlike the early intervention programs discussed above, do not have sufficient evaluation materials to suggest replication of efforts at this time. Instead, we recommend that well-funded and comprehensive pilot programs be implemented for the following purposes:

■ Development of comprehensive community schools with greatly expanded hours, sessions, and services. Where implemented, these projects should be run on a districtwide basis to have maximum impact and avoid the problem of stigmatization that may result from selecting only the most at-risk children for inclusion.

■ Development of well-equipped residential schools, properly funded, staffed, and ethnically enriched, to act as placement alternatives for children whose parents have had their parental rights terminated by court order.

Again, we must emphasize the value of properly conducted evaluations of pilot programs before large-scale implementation of these proposals. There is a vast literature regarding treatment and prevention programs, but the number of programs that have been adequately evaluated is minute. Therefore, we propose the creation of a limited number of well-funded major interventions with sufficient provision for adequate research design and long-term evaluation. Furthermore, we recommend that the U.S. Department of Justice coordinate with the U.S. Department of Education at the highest levels to ensure that the concerns of law enforcement are not only implemented in school curriculums, but that the concept of early childhood intervention as a fundamental component of law enforcement is accepted as part of basic educational policy nationwide.

Conclusion

We face the 21st century with the alarming prospect of ever-increasing juvenile and adult criminality, the continued disintegration of the family unit, and the continued decay of our inner cities. Our solutions must be as powerful and comprehensive as the problems they address. Because even the best prevention programs need considerable time to bear fruit, we have no choice but to immediately upgrade our law enforcement alternatives. Knowing full well the ultimate futility of law enforcement for a generation of children who lack elementary socialization and self-control, we are nonetheless obligated to detect and punish those who make life intolerable for others.

But this we know. The heart of any lastingly effective program to reduce delinquency and criminality and to increase the likelihood of effective deterrence necessarily involves the family and early childhood. Therefore, we advocate the expansion of early childhood intervention programs and the upgrading of Head Start. Beyond that, programs to establish adequate out-of-home placement (remedial residential schools and upgraded foster-care services) and programs to expand radically the scope of public education should be implemented as major pilot projects. The effectiveness of these pilot projects can thereafter be properly evaluated so that societal and educational policies can be intelligently planned and implemented during the next century.

The cost of this concept of a greatly expanded scope of public education will be enormous, but it is not without precedent. In the 1950's and 1960's we Americans, recognizing the need for higher education in our competition with the Soviet Union, proceeded to construct one of the greatest systems of colleges and universities in the world. Just such an effort is needed now for the lower and preschool grades to address the children most in need of our protection and care.

Notes

1. For example, homicide and manslaughter arrests for those under 18 years of age rose 60.1 percent from 1981 to 1990; arrests for aggravated assault and motor vehicle theft grew over 50 percent during the same time period. Federal Bureau of Investigation, *Uniform Crime Reports for the United States*. 1991. Cited in Yoshikawa, H. (1994) Prevention as Cumulative Protection; "Effects of Early Family Support and Education on Chronic Delinquency and its Risks," *Psychological Bulletin*, vol. 115:28–54.

2. Leitenberg, H. 1987. "Primary Prevention of Delinquency," in *Prevention of Delinquent Behavior*, Burchard and Burchard (eds.), p. 320.

3. Yoshikawa, supra, at 35.

4. Binder, A., G. Geis, and D. Bruce. 1988. *Juvenile Delinquency: Historical, Cultural and Legal Perspectives*. New York: Macmillan; Farrington, D.P., R. Loeber, D.S. Elliot, J.D. Hawkins, D.B. Kandel, M.W. Klein, J. McCord, D.C. Rose, and R.E. Trembly. 1990. "Advancing Knowledge About the Onset of Delinquency and Crime," in B.B. Lahey and A.E. Kazdin (eds.), *Advances in Clinical Child Psychology*, vol. 13:283–342. New York: Plenum Press; Hirschi, T. 1969. *The Causes of Delinquency*. Berkeley: University of California Press; and Wilson, J.Q., and G. Loury. 1987. *Families, Schools, and Delinquency Prevention*, p. vi.

5. Louber, R., and M. Stouthamer-Loeber. 1986. "Family Factors as Correlates and Predictors of Juvenile Conduct Problems and Delinquency," in M. Tony and N. Morris (eds.), *Crime and Justice; An Annual Review of Research*, vol. 7:29–150. Chicago: University of Chicago Press.

6. Basharov, D.J. 1987. "Giving the Juvenile Court a Preschool Education," in Wilson and Loury, supra, at 214; Wright and Wright. 1994. "A Policy Maker's Guide to Controlling Delinquency through Family Intervention," *Justice Quarterly*, vol. 11, no. 2:193; Loeber, R., and T.J. Dishion. 1983. "Early Predictors of Male Delinquency: A Review," *Psychological Bulletin*, vol. 94 (19):68–69.

7. Cohen, P., and J. Brook. 1987. "Family Factors Related to the Persistence of Psychopathology in Childhood and Adolescence," *Psychiatry*, vol. 50:332–345; Laub, J.H., and R.J. Sampson. 1988. "Unraveling Families and Delinquency: A Re-analysis of the Gluecks' Data." *Criminology*, vol. 26:355–380.

8. Loury, G. 1987. In Wilson and Loury, supra, at 6.

9. Farrington, D.P. 1987. "Early Precursors of Frequent Offending," in Wilson, J.Q., and G. Loury, supra, at 27–50.

10. Wolfgang, M.E., R.M. Figlio, and T. Sellin. 1972. *Delinquency in a Birth Cohort*. Chicago: University of Chicago Press; and West, D.J., and D.P. Farrington. 1977. *The Delinquent Way of Life*. New York: Crane Russak.

11. Wilson, J.Q., in Wilson and Loury, supra, at 300.

12. Rose, S.L., S.A. Rose, and Feldman. 1989. "Stability of Behavior Problems in Very Young Children," *Development and Psychopathology*, vol. 1:5–19.

13. Zigler, E.C., Taussig, and K. Black. 1992. "Early Childhood Intervention: A Promising Preventative for Juvenile Delinquency," *American Psychologist*, vol. 47:997–1065.

14. Yoshikawa, supra, at 37.

15. Beruetta-Clement, J.R., L.J. Schweinhardt, W.S. Barnett, A.S. Epstein, and D.P. Weikert. 1984. *Changed Lives: The Effects of the Perry Preschool Program on Youths Through Age 19*, Ypsilanti, MI: High/Scope Press.

16. Johnson, D.L., and T. Walker. 1987. "Primary Prevention of Behavior Problems in Mexican-American Children," *American Journal of Community Psychology*, vol. 15:375–385.

17. Lally, J.R., P.L. Mangione, A.S. Honig, and D.S. Wittner. "The Syracuse University Family Development Research Program: Long-Range Impact of Early Intervention with Low-Income Children and their Families," in D.R. Powell (ed.), *Annual Advances in Applied Developmental Psychology*, vol. 3:79–104, Norwood, NJ: Ablex.

18. Seitz, V., L.R. Rosenbaum, and Apfel. 1985. "Effects of Family Support Intervention; A Ten Year Follow-up," *Child Development*, vol. 56:376–391.

19. Kolvin, I., F.J.W. Miller, M. Fleeting, and P.S. Kolvin. 1988. "Social and Parenting Factors Affecting Criminal Offense Rates," *British Journal of Psychiatry*, vol. 152:80–90; Sameroff, A.J., and B.H. Fiese. 1990.

"Transactional Regulation and Early Intervention," S.J. Meisel and J.P. Shonkoff (eds.), *Handbook of Early Childhood Intervention*, 119–149. Cambridge, UK: Cambridge University Press.

20. Casto, G., and K. White. 1985. "The Efficacy of Early Intervention Programs with Environmentally At-Risk Infants," in M. Frank (ed.), *Infant Intervention Programs: Truths and Untruths*, 37–50, New York: Hayworth Press.

21. Zigler, E., and N. Hall. 1987. "The Implications of Early Intervention Efforts for the Primary Prevention of Juvenile Delinquency," in Wilson and Loury, supra, at 165.

22. Wilson, J.Q., supra, at 300.

23. Zigler and Hall, supra, at 173.

24. Kazdin. 1987. "Treatment of Anti-Social Behavior in Children, Current Status and Future Directions," *Psychological Bulletin*, vol. 1022:187–203; Rutter, M., and H. Gillen. 1983. *Juvenile Delinquency; Trends and Perspectives*. New York: Penguin Books; and Zigler, Taussig, and Black, supra, at 997–1,006.

25. Zigler, E., and M. Finn-Stevenson. 1989. "Child Care in America: From Problem to Solution," *Educational Policy*, vol. 3, no. 4:313–329; Weizel, R. "Remaking Schools to Fit Families for the 21st Century," *New York Times*, Feb. 13, 1994.

26. Besharov, supra, at 220.

27. Leitenberg, supra, at 323.

28. Ibid, at 319.

29. The cost of such a program remains a contentious issue among experts, with estimates of $20,000 to $60,000 per child per year. "Orphanages," *Newsweek*, Dec. 12, 1994, p. 30.

30. Leitenberg, supra, at 321.

31. Wright, W.E., and M.C. Dixon. 1977. "Community Prevention and Treatment of Juvenile Delinquency: A Review of Evaluation Studies," *Journal of Research in Crime and Delinquency*, vol. 14:35–67.

Drug Policy Options: Lessons From Three Epidemics

DRUG POLICY OPTIONS: LESSONS FROM THREE EPIDEMICS

Summary

Issues

Beginning with the heroin epidemic of the 1960's and continuing through the devastating crack epidemic, drug crises have regularly taken center stage in American politics and crime control policy. Through the 1980's, the central doctrine in U.S. drug policy has been "legalism." In this view, drug use challenges the established social order and moral foundations of authority. Drug policies have emphasized criminal penalties and deterrence over prevention and treatment as control mechanisms.

These drug policies have had a push-down-pop-up effect: the more pressure applied in one place, the more likely new problems were to arise in another. For example, criminal sanctions for low-level crack users have shifted resources away from treatment of such users, whose behaviors are vectors for HIV transmission through high-risk sexual activity.

The lessons from decades of legalistic drug policies suggest that deterrence strategies have not been successful in reducing drug use. Enforcement strategies have consumed resources, aggravated the health risks associated with drugs, and increased the levels of violence surrounding drug markets. Drug policy has also increased profits for drug sellers and attracted other young people into selling, as the exaggerated symbols of conspicuous consumption by dealers act as a siren for younger people. Severe sentencing laws applied broadly and indiscriminately have undermined, rather than reinforced, the moral authority of the law.

Policy recommendations

Policies need to focus on reducing the harmful consequences of drug use and place criminal penalties within a framework recognizing the scale of drug problems. Enforcement and prosecution should be used to disrupt mid- and upper-level trafficking, while treatment or alternative sanctions should be used to reduce drug demand among offenders whose drug use has propelled them into the criminal justice system. The cornerstone of a new drug policy should be to increase alcohol and drug treatment opportunities at all stages of the criminal justice system.

- **Treatment-oriented drug courts.** Continued experimentation with treatment-oriented drug courts should be encouraged. A potentially powerful model for linking the treatment/public health system to the criminal justice process, these courts should continue to be developed and evaluated for their long-term effectiveness. The risk of unnecessarily widening the net of social control can be minimized through the use of appropriate eligibility and screening criteria and comprehensive, clinically based assessment.

- **Alcohol and other drug (AOD) treatment.** Access to AOD treatment and public health services should be encouraged at all stages of the criminal justice process. Accordingly, opportunities for effective treatment interventions during the pretrial period, probation-supervised treatment, treatment under a community corrections model, and prison- or jail-based treatment should be studied and encouraged. All criminal-justice-based treatment services should consider the provision of aftercare services to provide a treatment continuum.

- **Community mobilization.** Communities can effectively mobilize to disrupt drug markets and deter drug users. Many case studies have depicted the benefits of community policing with respect to reducing the size and scope of drug markets, but few systematic studies have appeared that could corroborate this effect. However, this approach seems more likely to support the linkage of treatment and public health services to law enforcement than traditional anti-drug enforcement approaches.

- **Disaggregated prevention strategies.** Prevention strategies should be disaggregated for specific drugs and populations. They should be built from an understanding of the mechanisms through which individuals acquire information about drugs and make decisions about their use. The lessons of drug epidemics are that information about drug use rules and dangers is spread informally from credible sources and learned from social experiences; normative changes in drug use patterns are influenced weakly by legal threats.

- **Target drug treatment.** The concentration of high-rate and -risk drug use among a small segment of the population suggests that treatment efforts should be targeted to them. Many of these individuals are in prison, and their criminality is closely (and perhaps causally) linked to drug problems. Cost arguments alone make inprison treatment a necessary part of an overall strategy for drug control, but the opportunity to reduce criminality together with drug problems is a compelling reason for funding inmates' treatment.

- **Alternatives to incarceration.** Citing the need to alleviate overcrowding and prioritize prison space for violent offenders, several governors and State legislatures have recommended that penal statutes permit the sentencing of nonviolent drug offenders to nonincarcerative punishments. Expansion of viable alternatives to incarceration, however, have been stifled by fiscal restraints. Incentives must be created to sustain States' efforts to create alternatives, such as supervision programs involving urinalysis, outpatient and residential drug treatment, or health and employment programs.

- **Harm-reduction model.** Treating drug addiction as the chronic disease that it is enables legal institutions to achieve realistic and attainable goals. From this perspective, a harm reduction model becomes the framework for policy. Myriad forms of harm can be addressed by selective application of criminal "pressure" to divert users into treatment that may eventually return them to families and/or employment.

- **Buyer-seller interactions.** Supply-side strategies should focus on interactions between buyers and sellers, making drug purchases more difficult by increasing search time for buyers and decreasing revenues for sellers. International interventions and interdictions at the top of the domestic distribution system should have low priority compared to point-of-sale efforts to reduce available supplies.

- **Local concerns.** Enforcement, treatment, and health care are local matters, and responsibility for enforcement and funding of drug policy should be shifted downward to the States.

- **Federal concerns.** The development of knowledge, technology, data, and information should be organized within a policy infrastructure at the Federal level.

DRUG POLICY OPTIONS:
LESSONS FROM THREE EPIDEMICS

Background

For more than 30 years, the United States has experienced a succession of drug crises. Beginning with the heroin epidemic of the 1960's and continuing through the cocaine and devastating crack epidemics of the 1980's, drug crises have regularly taken center stage in American politics and crime control policy. During the 1980's, deepening public anxiety about drug problems led to drug control choices that have taken a deep hold on the legal and social landscape of nearly every segment of American society. From drug testing in the workplace to incarceration in the Nation's overcrowded prisons, the United States has embarked on unprecedented social experiments to control the use of drugs.

The central doctrine in U.S. drug policy throughout these crises has been "legalism" (Zimring and Hawkins, 1992). In this doctrine, drug use challenges the established social order and the moral foundations of authority.[1] Drug policies have emphasized criminal penalties and deterrence as mechanisms to control drug problems, with prevention and treatment receiving a lower priority and far less funding. The increased use of criminal justice resources was designed to achieve three interrelated aims: reduce drug demand by deterring would-be users, reduce drug supply by disrupting street-level markets, and reduce street violence that is the by-product of illegal drug use. The policy responses required low incarceration thresholds for violations of drug laws and a high likelihood of arrest for drug use and sales through extensive street-level enforcement. To accomplish this, resources were diverted from prevention and treatment toward enforcement and incarceration.

These policy choices have been made in an atmosphere of intense concern but often without careful conceptual development or policy analysis. Perhaps most importantly, we have yet to measure the consequences and returns from the policy choices we have made. Today, an opportunity exists for such evaluation and rethinking of these policy choices. Like the epidemics that preceded it, the crack epidemic has run its natural course. The crisis that accompanied the onset and peak of the crack epidemic has subsided even though significant drug problems remain.[2] There is now empirical information and rational perspective on many policy initiatives undertaken during the mobilization of the past decade and also from lessons to be learned from earlier drug crises. This allows us to highlight those policies with promise and those whose limits were quickly reached. It also provides a context in which to formulate a coherent drug policy framework where specific initiatives make sense and where policies can synergistically achieve meaningful reductions in drug problems.

Challenges to Drug Policy: What Not To Do

We frame these policy choices in the context of several challenges that have emerged from the drug control experiments of the past decade. The challenges reflect the lessons learned from the realities of drug problems and the experiences of implementing large-scale mobilization of legal and social resources.

First, the experiment of mass incarceration over the past decade suggests the limits of deterrence-based strategies for controlling large-scale drug problems. The sharp increases in incarceration rates have resulted in limited success in reducing the use or availability of drugs (see, for detailed analyses, Kleiman, 1992; Zimring and Hawkins, 1992; Moore, 1993; Reuter, 1991). The use of precious criminal justice resources has not brought returns from either market disruption or demand reduction. The lesson of the past decade lies in recognizing the limits of legal institutions and criminal justice systems in dealing with drug use. Epidemics such as the recent cocaine, crack, and heroin epidemics suggest that societal drug problems occur on a scale that exceeds the limited capacity of the criminal justice system. To mobilize legal institutions on a scale that would match these drug crises is not practical in a complex society with multiple policy demands and declining economic resources. It also raises problems for the consensus on law and the importance of fairness (Moore, 1993; Tonry, 1995). A more realistic strategy would recognize that effective drug control requires reciprocity between criminal justice and other interventions, including public health or drug treatment.

Second, recurrent drug problems place extraordinary burdens on police, courts, and communities. During the 1980's, police efforts were targeted toward mass arrests that created organizational burdens to sustain them. Police corruption from drug enforcement became a recurring management problem that threatened morale and public confidence in the police. The quality of justice in the courts was compromised by the crush of caseloads and the pressures to move calendars (Wisotsky, 1990; Belenko, 1993). Prisons suffered in two ways: overcrowding and the emergence of a new generation of inmates that posed challenges for prison management and security.[3] Although communities demanded increased enforcement to rid themselves of drug dealers, many residents resented what they perceived as the aggressive enforcement of unfair laws that were disproportionately targeted toward minority citizens. These policies served to increase disrespect for and resistance to the law among many citizens (Reuter, 1991). Judges resisted mandatory sentencing statutes that stripped them of their discretion in sentencing, further undermining the public's confidence in the same laws that drug policy was trying to reinforce.

Third, drug policy is further challenged by its interdependency with health, crime control, and other social policies. Drug policy often has a push-down-pop-up effect: the more we put pressure in one place, the more likely we are to experience new problems in another. Thus, for example, as we continue to limit severely the distribution of clean syringes, we increase the health risks of HIV transmission among intravenous heroin and cocaine users. Or criminal sanctions for low-level crack dealers focus resources away from treatment of crack and cocaine users whose behaviors provide vectors for HIV transmission through high-risk sexual activity. Or successful interdiction of marijuana imports encourages domestic growers to develop higher potency crops that pose significantly greater health threats (Kleiman, 1992).[4] In contrast, the relatively

low-scale efforts to treat drug users in the criminal justice system exposes untreated defendants to the risks of family disruption, poor health outcomes, exposure to violence in illegal drug markets, and other social deficits. For example, one of the important policy lessons of the past decade is that incarceration of adolescents relegates them to a lifetime of poor job outcomes and persistent involvement in criminality (Freeman, 1992), yet the expansion of drug enforcement resulted in an increase in the number of young people incarcerated and spiraling problems of crime and unemployment.

Fourth, drug policy debates have been competitions between supply-side hawks and demand-reduction doves. The hawks focus on reducing the availability of illegal drugs on the street through interventions up and down the distribution system. Their arguments are buttressed by inconsistent evidence of treatment effectiveness, the immediacy of drug problems, and the incapacitating effects of incarceration. Theirs is an urgent and simple message, in contrast to the social logic of the doves: deterrence does not work; prevention and treatment have been underfunded; and drug problems are social in their origins and require social solutions. The debate has turned—and stalled—on the question of the extent of drug use and drug problems (Reuter, 1991). This reflects the legalism doctrine that informs much of drug policy, where drug use (and not its consequences) is the concern of policymakers. However, legalistic policies have not succeeded in reducing either drug use or drug problems.

When the policy focus shifts to the societal burdens and consequences of drug use, as it has in European countries, other policy frameworks become possible. Specifically, alternative policy frameworks are needed that recognize the possibly adverse effects of legalistic drug policy and that focus on reducing the risk of drug harm rather than the prevalence of drug use. Policies that consider risk shifting (from legal to social domains, from supply side to demand side) and comparative-risk-and-advantage analysis afford the greatest potential for more than symbolic gains in efforts to control drug use.

In sum, the lessons from three decades of legalistic drug policies suggest deterrence strategies have not been successful in reducing drug use. In fact, their adverse effects have intensified certain health and social risks of drug use. There is little evidence of either general or specific deterrent effects (Fagan, 1994; Zimring and Hawkins, 1992; Reuter, 1991). Enforcement strategies have consumed resources, aggravated the health risks associated with drugs, and increased the levels of violence surrounding drug markets. Drug policy through the 1980's also has resulted in increased profits for drug sellers, which have attracted other young people into selling as the exaggerated symbols of conspicuous consumption by dealers act as a siren's song for younger people (Fagan, 1992). The application of severe sentencing laws with a broad and nondiscriminating reach have undermined rather than reinforced the moral authority of the law among many citizens and judges. In the next section, we apply these lessons to form drug policies that assign a strategic and complementary role for criminal law and for the Nation's legal institutions.

Policy Concepts

The lessons of the past decade and the legacies of policies formed in preceding decades suggest principles for informed policy for the future. The burden on the criminal justice system created by reliance on criminal sanctions for drug offenses, together with the general consensus among criminal justice policy-makers and practitioners that this policy has not accomplished its goals, suggest that new approaches must be considered and encouraged.

First, we encourage policies that focus on reducing the risks and harmful consequences of drug use with an emphasis on demand-side policies to shrink illegal drug markets. Policies should pursue realistic and attainable goals for reducing the harms that accrue from drug use. Criminal penalties should be part of a broader policy framework that recognizes the scale of drug problems. This policy approach does not necessarily mean that enforcement efforts should be ignored or downplayed. Instead, a bifurcated drug policy is needed that distinguishes among offenders in terms of their drug involvement. Enforcement and prosecution should be used to disrupt middle- and upper-level trafficking, while treatment or alternative sentencing interventions should be used to reduce drug demand among low-level dealers with drug problems. Diversion and referrals should focus on reduction of drug use among offenders whose under-

lying drug problems have impelled their entry into the criminal justice system.

Second, the inclusion of public health and other social policies will expand the forms of social control that can reinforce the goals of criminal justice interventions. There is an important role for criminal penalties, but the challenge is to use criminal penalties strategically and reciprocally with other interventions. Drug offenders are at high risk for infectious disease, so effective referral and intervention also becomes a public health issue. The high prevalence of HIV infection, tuberculosis, sexually transmitted diseases, and hepatitis among criminal offenders increases the urgency of fostering new policies that allow broader public health interventions at all stages of criminal justice processing. Two other key parts of the policy equation are education and prevention programs and increased economic opportunities, especially in poor urban areas.

One policy implication of this approach is that we need to greatly improve current collaborations between criminal justice and alcohol and other drug (AOD) treatment systems. This includes both increased opportunities for collaboration as well as making such interactions more effective and meaningful. We recognize that important steps in this direction have already been taken, as illustrated by the recent development of treatment diversion drug courts. However, the number of drug-involved offenders entering drug courts is a very small proportion of those in need of AOD treatment. There is a growing need, already recognized by the U.S. Department of Justice and the U.S. Department of Health and Human Services, to seek collaborative efforts, multidisciplinary approaches, and meaningful community involvement to address long-term problems of crime and substance abuse with more effective solutions. This will require a shift in the allocation of criminal justice system resources away from harmful or counterproductive policies, such as the imprisonment of nonviolent drug abusers or low-level drug sellers, toward strategies with greater effectiveness and long-term impact on drug abuse. It will be necessary to implement sometimes politically sensitive shifts in resources in favor of such interventions as AOD treatment programs, diversion, and alternatives to incarceration and away from law enforcement, prison, and jail for drug-involved nonviolent offenders. Experience has shown that there is consistent, broad public support for AOD treatment for these types of offenders as well as strong support in the law enforcement and judicial communities.

The cornerstone of a new drug policy that can more effectively break the drug-crime cycle is the increase in AOD treatment opportunities at all stages of the criminal justice system. Although some offenders can reduce or eliminate their drug use without treatment, most need some sort of external pressure to enter and remain in treatment. We know that sanctions in and of themselves will not reduce drug-related crime, nor will punitive sanctions deter drug sales or drug use. It is a basic principle of human behavior that punishment by itself will not change behavior; opportunities and rewards for competing prosocial behaviors must be offered. Treatment drug courts recognize this principle, and this may account for their apparent success in channeling offenders into treatment.

Finally, a realistic, effective, and balanced approach should not be hampered by inflexible and punitive laws that limit the ability of prosecutors and judges to allow treatment interventions. Accordingly, we recommend against mandatory minimum sentences for nonviolent drug-involved offenders with a concomitant increase in prosecutorial and judicial discretion.

Policy Options

Demand Reduction Strategies

Since 1980, drug laws have been used as the primary mechanism for demand reduction among drug users. Moral injunction and deterrence inform this perspective. However, the inelasticity of demand in the face of mass incarceration of drug offenders suggests that alternative methods of demand reduction be considered. One of the reasons for recommending a policy emphasis on demand reduction is the growing evidence that the marginal (formal) deterrence effects of criminal penalties are small. Instead, we recommend strategies that focus on the (informal) mechanisms by which individuals reduce their drug use.

Move ahead with experiments on drug courts. Continued experimentation with treatment-oriented drug courts should be encouraged. These courts arose out of local, grassroots frustration with the inability of

prevailing punitive anti-drug policies to reduce drug-related crime. They are also part of important trends in the criminal courts: the shifting roles of court participants; a changing view of offenders as individuals requiring individual attention rather than simply as criminal cases; a multidisciplinary, case-management approach to responding to offenders; and increased community involvement and sensitivity toward community concerns in the court process. The drug courts reflect a broader, longer range approach to drug-related crime, emphasizing the solution of underlying problems rather than just the repeated punishment of criminal acts. They represent a potentially powerful model for linking the treatment and public health systems to the criminal justice process, and continued development and evaluation of their long-term effectiveness should be strongly encouraged by the Federal Government.

One potential downside to treatment drug courts and other diversion or alternative sentencing programs is the risk of unnecessarily widening the net of social control. Like any intervention strategy, the focus should be on those individuals who will be most responsive to interventions. This risk can be minimized through appropriate eligibility and screening criteria along with comprehensive and clinically based assessment for underlying drug problems and jail-boundness.

Minimize harm: Improve linkages with drug treatment and public health and make treatment the first resort. Access to AOD treatment and public health services should be encouraged at all stages of the criminal justice process. Accordingly, opportunities for effective treatment interventions during the pretrial period, probation-supervised treatment, treatment under a community corrections model, and prison- or jail-based treatment should be studied and encouraged. Finally, all criminal-justice-based treatment services should consider the provision of aftercare services to provide a continuum of treatment and other services following release from jail or prison after criminal justice supervision has ended.

Capitalize on communities. There are strong conceptual and practical reasons to invest in communities as a form of drug control, and growing evidence that communities can effectively mobilize to disrupt drug markets and deter drug users (Currie, 1993).[5]

Community policing has received much attention and support in recent years, and the police-community relationship is a critical issue in drug policy. There are many case studies that illustrate the benefits of community policing with respect to reducing the size and scope of drug markets, but few systematic studies.[6] Although evidence of its effect on reducing the demand for drugs and its impact on the criminal justice system is still not available, this approach seems to be more likely to support the linkage of treatment and public health services to law enforcement than traditional anti-drug enforcement approaches that rely on undercover narcotics officers to disrupt street drug markets.

Get serious about prevention. More research is needed about how to make prevention and education effective. Prevention should be disaggregated for specific drugs and specific populations. Prevention strategies should be built from our understanding of the mechanisms through which individuals acquire information about drugs and make decisions about their use. Scary messages about the harms of drugs from noncredible sources are not effective for a heterogeneous population of current and would-be drug users.[7] Instead, the lessons of drug epidemics since the 1960's are that: (1) information about the dangers and rules of drug use are spread informally from credible sources, (2) the dangers of drug use are learned from direct or indirect but social (not legal) experiences, and (3) normative changes in drug use patterns are influenced weakly by legal threats. Prevention experiments are sorely needed, as is the political "time" to see these experiments through to their conclusion. These should be disaggregated by age, social location, and type of drug.

Expand drug treatment in prisons. The concentration of high-rate and high-risk drug use among a small segment of the population suggests that concentrated treatment efforts should be targeted at this population. Many high-rate, high-risk drug users are in prison, and their criminality is closely (and perhaps causally) linked to drug problems. The cost arguments alone make treatment a necessary part of an overall strategy for drug control, but opportunities to reduce criminality together with drug problems makes in-prison treatment a strong candidate for funding. There is limited but growing evidence of potential gains from this approach. Serious experimentation and research are needed to build a social technology that relies on the "push" of criminal sanctions to make gains in treatment.

Fund alternatives to incarceration. Several governors and State legislatures, most notably New York and Florida, have started to rethink the policy of mandatory minimums for nonviolent drug offenders. Citing the need to alleviate overcrowding and prioritize prison space for violent offenders, they have recommended that penal code statutes permit the sentencing of nonviolent drug offenders to nonincarcerative punishments. However, judges are likely to resist nonincarcerative sentences when the alternatives are weak. That is the case as fiscal limits negate the expansion of alternatives to incarceration (ATI) beyond their current small scale. These vary widely and can meet the supervision and treatment needs of a wide range of drug offenders. Any serious effort to avoid the adverse (expensive) consequences of incarceration will need a network of viable alternative sentencing options.

One way to achieve the shifting of funds to ATI programs is to provide incentives for local government to create and fill these programs. Subsidy programs, created decades ago as mechanisms to avoid "dumping" of offenders by local governments into State facilities, were successful in a number of jurisdictions that were intent on reducing their prison populations. States typically set a maximum for each county and awarded funds from a community corrections pool to localities on a prorated basis for the number of prison remands below the maximum. The subsidies often were used to establish community corrections programs or to enhance probation services. The same logic can be applied in the current context to support intensive supervision programs involving urinalysis, outpatient or residential drug treatment, and programs that address health or employment concerns. If the excessive use of incarceration for drug offenders is to be discontinued, incentives must be created to sustain the efforts of States to create and utilize alternatives to incarceration.

Reduce the harms from drug use. The focus on deterrence of drug use has left untouched spreading health harms caused by illegal drug use. Drug addiction is a chronic disease, albeit neither an infectious nor a contagious one. It should be treated from the perspective of chronic disease, helping us to achieve a set of realistic and attainable policy goals that focus on isolating causal dynamics and risk factors and to develop appropriate interventions. There is little evidence that drug addiction can be deterred through the threat of legal sanctions, and policies that make punishment the first resort set unrealistic and unachievable goals. An approach rooted in the reduction of the harms and public health risks of drug use will place legal institutions in a role where they are no longer burdened with unachievable missions. Thus containment of the harms of drug use, while strategically intervening on problematic drug use, is the essence of a harm-reduction model that can become a framework for policy.

Several communities with extensive heroin abuse problems have experimented successfully with needle exchanges to control the spread of HIV infection. Using careful criteria based on need, policies encouraging needle exchange help address the harms of drug use while providing opportunities to control use itself through referrals. Similarly, encouraging women users to seek medical care while pregnant (instead of threatening them with incarceration) will identify soon-to-be newborns at risk for low birth weight and other birth defects. These children, who grow up at risk for delinquency and violence, also are at risk for in utero addiction and addiction at birth. There are myriad other forms of harm that can be addressed by the selective application of criminal "pressure." Examples include the diversion of users into treatment to encourage their eventual return to their families and employment to encourage users to pursue lower-risk forms of drug use that minimize health and social harms.

Supply reduction strategies. Drug laws also have been used to reduce the supply of illegal drugs to consumers, to increase their street price, and to limit their availability to the average consumer. Supply-side policies have been implemented at all levels of the distribution chain, from production in foreign countries through importation and distribution systems involving wholesalers and street retailers. Supply-side policy assumes that both prices and demand for illegal drugs are elastic. The set of strategies that make up supply-side policy attempts to achieve marginal reductions in the price and availability of drugs, and the effects of these efforts, are enough to discourage at least some drug use.

The record from these efforts has been decidedly mixed. There have been successes either in reducing availability or increasing prices, but these gains have been short-lived. The reductions were temporary or small. For example, the number of heroin addicts in the United States has remained steady at about 250,000 people for nearly two decades after peaking at 500,000 people in the early 1970's. Drug epidemics come and go. There is little reliable evidence about street prices or the amount of drugs consumed to allow us to attribute drug-market behaviors to supply-side policies, but we should question the effectiveness of supply-side policies if drug consumption does not decline following their implementation (Moore, 1993).

However, supply-side policy must continue to be part of drug policy. There are several policy questions to be addressed in determining how best to use policy options on this side. First is the decision about where on the supply chain market disruption tactics should be focused. If demand is inelastic relative to price, there can be little justification for supply-side policies, but this is a narrow view in many regards. While inelasticity claims may be true for addicts, they may not be true for irregular consumers whose market behavior is more rationally oriented. Inelasticity also suggests that there are purely econometric effects on prices and, therefore, on consumer behavior. It is more likely that supply-side interventions will influence other dimensions of consumer behaviors and decisions, such as risk assessment and search time. We attend to these possibilities by suggesting the wise use of police resources to change market dynamics (apart from prices).

Where to intervene. Until recently, there was little differentiation in supply reduction policies regarding point of distribution. There is a complex and flexible distribution system for drugs that involves producers, transporters, importers, wholesalers, and local distribution networks. However, current efforts to interdict imports are indistinguishable in their priority from efforts to increase arrests of low-level drug dealers. This makes no sense, and priorities must be set.

Policies targeted toward producers outside the United States are high-cost, low-payoff ideas. The production of drugs is a political, economic phenomenon that is not easily amenable to intervention. Like domestic supply-side interventions, there are questions of scale that are not easily addressed through periodic crop destruction or disruption of remote processing facilities.[8] In this country, supply reduction tends to drive street prices slightly up. Because heroin and cocaine demand seems to be somewhat inelastic, supply reduction will cause an increase in street crimes (necessary to sustain drug consumption) and an increase in dealer revenues. A more lucrative market will continue to expand as newcomers are attracted to what appears to be a profitable market. Accordingly, policies that involve international interventions should receive a low priority.

Similarly, efforts to locate and convict various "Mr. Bigs" in cities throughout the United States have high costs relative to payoffs. Drug indicators suggest the intractability of imports and domestic supplies to such domestic interdictions, despite widely spaced, highly publicized seizures. So-called "kingpins" (and, increasingly, "queenpins") are quickly replaced by individuals within their own organizations if not by competitors. Nevertheless, there is an important symbolic value in efforts to interdict supplies overseas, at the borders, and at the upper levels of the distribution chain. These efforts reinforce the illegality of drug use, express intolerance for drug dealing, and reassure a public still anxious about drugs that efforts continue to disrupt supply systems.

*The priority assigned to international interventions and interdictions at the upper levels of the domestic distribution system should be low relative to point-of-sale efforts to reduce supplies available to us*ers.

The principle driving the decision about where to focus supply-side policies should address the simultaneity of supply and demand factors. While interdictions tend to increase prices for a short period of time, demand remains constant even when prices fluctuate (Warner, 1993).[9] Demand is inelastic with respect to price, but not with respect to other factors that we might call the "buying context." We suggest instead that supply-side interventions focus on consumer markets and market interactions. This does not mean that

we encourage street-level crackdowns aimed at jailing drug retailers. Crackdowns involving mass arrest have time-limited effects on drug selling (Vera Institute, 1992; Tonry, 1995). They simply shift buyers and sellers from neighborhood to neighborhood and clog the courts and compromise the quality of justice for both prosecution and defense. Often, crackdowns may simply drive markets indoors, out of the public eye, but with little lasting effect on consumer behavior.

Supply-side strategies should focus on interactions between buyers and sellers, making drug purchases more difficult by increasing search time for buyers and decreasing revenues for sellers.

We suggest that supply-side strategies focus on disrupting local markets, ensuring that they do not become institutionalized so that customers can regard them as a consumer convenience. When drugs are part of the marketplace where consumer interactions take place, the markets enjoy the ordinary economic protections of consumer behavior. Demand is constant and encourages a supply chain. But when markets are disrupted and unstable, consumers must endure a variety of inconveniences that increase the intangible costs of drugs. Strategies that encourage local market disruption should focus less on criminal enforcement than on using police to establish obstacles to consumers wishing to make purchases. This requires a detailed knowledge of the features of drug markets that encourage or discourage buying and which of these features can be modified to reduce harmful consequences if not actual use. This strategy is highly localized, with immediate payoffs focused on supplier-consumer interactions.

Who should intervene? The second question concerns the allocation between Federal and local policing in carrying out supply-side drug controls. The key issues involve the allocation of responsibility for setting policy, paying for it, and carrying it out. These decisions also occur in the context of political concerns about the extent of government in local crime control policy and about how to effectively spend a shrinking supply of Federal dollars.

Large-scale Federal block grant programs have short lives and ultimately few lasting effects on policy, programs, or the problems they are intended to resolve. Their impacts are diffuse and uneven. One of their primary failings is that they do not create cumulative knowledge that can lead to informed and well-evaluated policies or strategies. However, the creation of a policy infrastructure with carefully defined missions can influence policy in a lasting way (Zimring and Hawkins, 1992). Despite the current talk about block grants to diversify and localize funding decisions, history is clear that block grants come and go, and they have had shorter and shorter half-lives since the 1960's. The lessons of the Law Enforcement Assistance Administration teach us much about the limits of block grants, whether to States or localities.

The responsibility for enforcement and funding of drug policy should be shifted downward to the States. The development of knowledge, technology, data, and information should be organized within a policy infrastructure at the Federal level.

Laws are enforced locally, drug users are treated locally, and health problems are addressed locally. There is diversity in the nature of drug problems within and across States. This suggests a shifting of responsibility downward together with funding. What then should the Federal Government do? The Government should conduct test marketing of ideas and strategies through experimentation, disseminate systematic knowledge, coordinate technology, and ensure that information is standardized, accurate, and up-to-date. From this foundation of knowledge, effective policies can be fashioned.

A Research Agenda

The research agenda involves the careful testing of these policy options, including initiatives in the following four areas:

■ Analyzing harm reduction strategies and careful testing using systemic models.

■ Conducting policy experiments on drug courts and "true" diversion models.

■ Improving treatment and criminal justice linkages.

■ Understanding consumer behavior in drug markets.

Experimentation is critically important. Drug policy has been made in its absence, yet its importance for the wise expenditure of scarce funds is obvious. We

encourage the replication of the current experiments on the District of Columbia Drug Court, as well as treatment experiments and other research efforts that carefully test policy assumptions. Consumer research is also important. Understanding the social and psychological processes that give rise to maturation and desistance from drug use should inform the design of policy.

Research should help set attainable goals for drug policy. To avoid setting unrealistic goals is critically important for maintaining the integrity and moral authority of legal institutions, for their failure to control drug problems has raised serious criticisms with constitutional implications. This is a lesson of the past three decades and a problem we can avoid with some political will.

Notes

1. The Office of National Drug Control Policy (ONDCP) strategy represents trends and assumptions that have informed drug policy nationwide for more than two decades. By stating drug problems in moral terms, or mala in se (Hughes, 1983), drug use and selling were defined as dual problems of legal transgressions. First, the strategy developed by ONDCP (1989) assumed that all drugs are bad and that none is more dangerous than another. Taking or selling illegal drugs is a socially deviant act whose social and health consequences are sufficiently harmful to merit State control and intervention. Second, since drugs are illegal, taking or selling them undermines the law, and by extension, the social order of laws. This position is termed "legalism" by Zimring and Hawkins (1992), who distinguish it from other views that are more functional regarding the public health and econometric (cost-benefit) consequences of drugs.

2. A core of high-rate cocaine and crack users remains active, while the prevalence of casual hard-drug use has declined. Drug use declined dramatically in the 1980's, according to the National Institute on Drug Abuse. The number of users of any illegal drug dropped by 37 percent, from 23 million in 1985 to 14 million in 1988. The FBI's Uniform Crime Reports show that homicides, many of them related to drug transactions, peaked in 1991 but have declined steadily since then. However, the percentage of

arrestees testing positive for cocaine or heroin has remained steady at the high rates first reached in the mid-1980's (Kleiman, 1992; Zimring and Hawkins, 1992). At the same time, the high rates of lethal violence that accompanied the emergence of crack markets a decade ago have now subsided. There are indications of the re-emergence of heroin as a popular addictive drug, but the prevalence of heroin among arrestees and in emergency room admission remains low compared with cocaine (Kleiman, 1992). Rates of marijuana use among adolescents have increased slightly since their lowest points in the mid-1980's, while alcohol remains the most persistent problem among psychoactive substances for both adults and adolescents (National Institute on Drug Abuse, 1994).

3. Many policies actually worsened the problems they intended to solve. For example, over half the admissions to California prisons in 1988 were technical parole violations of parolees who tested positive for illegal drugs (Messinger, 1990, cited in Zimring and Hawkins, 1992). Formal punishments were limited to incarceration or virtually nothing, as the public demanded (and received) the most extreme forms of punishment for drug offenders. As a result, the availability of treatment and rigorous forms of community supervision declined as funds shifted toward case processing and the incarceration of drug offenders.

4. It is not clear whether the carcinogens in the domestic crop are greater than in the imports. However, head shop bans have shifted smoking from products using water filtration to rolled joints. But water dissolved most of the carcinogenic material from marijuana cigarettes, material that is ingested in its rolled form. See Kleiman, 1992.

5. There is a wide variety of citizen initiatives that illustrate this point. Groups operating within neighborhoods have used a wide range of tactics to address drug problems. Perhaps most interesting is that the tactics almost always involve strengthening the communities by dealing with problems beyond those of drugs. The collaboration of communities and police is a common theme in these efforts. Communities turned to police to address both the immediate problems of drug markets and other criminogenic conditions in their neighborhoods, but the groups also addressed

political problems such as the availability of health services, recreation, and housing problems to reduce the risks of drug use and dealing in their areas.

6. The evaluation of Chicago's community policing experiment will provide systematic evidence of its effects on drug crimes and other offenses.

7. Evaluations of the Nation's largest effort, the Drug Abuse Resistance Education (D.A.R.E.) program, shows limited effectiveness as do other evaluations of prevention programs that use law enforcement officers as deliverers of anti-drug messages. See, for example, Rosenbaum et al., 1994.

8. The growing and refinery areas within producing countries are not often subject to civil authority, and domestic interdictions within those areas risk civil unrest. Moreover, drug incomes have become institutionalized in the economies and political interests of many producer nations, and U.S. dollars funneled to foreign authorities to suppress exports become easy plunder for corrupt officials. See, for example, Edmundo Morales, *Cocaine: White Gold Rush in Peru* (1989) for an idea of the scale and institutionalization of the drug economies of a producer nation that is intricately tied to international distribution networks.

Peter Reuter has observed that drug policy complicates our foreign policy. In the 1980's, U.S. relations with Pakistan focused on the Soviet presence in neighboring Afghanistan. Efforts to control opium production were compromised by higher policy priorities assigned to containing Soviet militarism. Policies designed to reduce heroin and marijuana production in Mexico have failed to stem either production or transshipments within that country, and they have increased the power of traffickers and their influence on Mexico's domestic politics.

9. We really should say here "to the best of our knowledge." The data problems in cocaine prices at either the retail or wholesale level are quite significant. Prices vary across cities and time, and because import figures and seizure data are likely to be distorted, price estimates should be viewed cautiously.

References

Belenko, Steven, 1993, *Crack and the Evolution of Anti-Drug Policy.* Greenwich, CT: Greenwood Press.

Currie, Eliot, 1993, *Reckoning: Drugs, the Cities, and the American Future.* New York: Hill and Wang.

Fagan, Jeffrey, 1992, "Drug selling and illicit income in distressed neighborhoods: The economic lives of street-level drug users and dealers." In *Drugs, Crime and Social Isolation: Barriers to Urban Opportunity,* edited by A.V. Harrell and G.E. Peterson. Washington, DC: Urban Institute Press.

_____1994, "Do criminal sanctions deter drug offenders?" In *Drugs and Criminal Justice: Evaluating Public Policy Initiatives,* edited by D. MacKenzie and C. Uchida. Newbury Park, CA: Sage.

Freeman, Richard B., 1992, "Crime and the economic status of disadvantaged young men." In *Urban Labor Markets and Job Opportunity,* edited by G.E. Peterson and W. Vroman. Washington, DC: Urban Institute Press.

Hughes, Graham, 1983, "The concept of crime." In *The Encyclopedia of Crime and Justice,* edited by S. Kalish. New York: MacMillan.

Kleiman, Mark A.R., 1992, *Against Excess: Drug Policy for Results.* New York: Basic Books.

Moore, Mark H., 1993, "Drugs, law and justice." In *Confronting Drug Policy: Illicit Drugs in a Free Society,* edited by R. Bayer and G.M. Oppenheimer. New York: Cambridge University Press.

Morales, Edmundo, 1989, *Cocaine: White Gold Rush in Peru.* Tuscon: University of Arizona Press.

Office of National Drug Control Policy, 1989, *National Drug Control Strategy.* Washington, DC: The White House.

Reuter, Peter, 1991, "On the consequences of toughness." In *Searching for Alternatives: Drug-Control Policy in the United States,* edited by M.B. Krauss and E.P. Lazear. Stanford, CA: Hoover Press.

Rosenbaum, Dennis P., Robert Flewelling, S.L. Bailey, C.L. Ringwalt and Deanna L. Wilkinson, 1994, "Cops in the Classroom: A Longitudinal Evaluation of Drug Abuse Resistance Education (DARE)." *Journal of Research in Crime and Delinquency* 31: 3–31.

Sviridoff, Michelle, Susan Sadd, Rick Curtis, and Randolph Grinc, 1992, "The Neighborhood Effects of Street-Level Drug Enforcement," Final Report, National Institute of Justice Grant 89–IJ–CX–0056. New York: Vera Institute.

Tonry, Michael, 1995, *Malign Neglect.* New York: Oxford University Press.

Warner, Kenneth E., 1993, "Legalizing drugs: Lessons from (and about) economics." In *Confronting Drug Policy: Illicit Drugs in a Free Society,* edited by R. Bayer and G.M. Oppenheimer. New York: Cambridge University Press.

Wisotsky, Steven, 1990, *Beyond the War on Drugs* (2nd edition). Buffalo, NY: Prometheus Books.

Zimring, Franklin E., and Gordon Hawkins, 1992, *The Search for Rational Drug Control Policy.* New York: Cambridge University Press.

Drugs and the Community

DRUGS AND THE RURAL COMMUNITY

Summary

Issues

Although it has been relatively ignored in research and policy, the issue of illegal drugs in rural America is considered among the most pressing problems facing rural police. Illicit rural drug activities include consumption, production, and transshipment.

Overall, rural and urban youths are equally likely to be drug users, but cocaine and crack cocaine use is generally lower in rural areas, whereas the use of inhalants and stimulants is higher. Circumstantial evidence suggests that the link between drug use and violence is weaker in rural areas than in cities (rural areas have substantially less violent crime—except for domestic violence, for which urban and rural rates are about equal). Data indicate that alcohol use is a much greater problem in rural areas, and driving under the influence (DUI) is a serious rural problem, with the arrest rate double that in urban areas.

An estimated 25–50 percent of the marijuana consumed in the U.S. is domestically grown, and nearly all commercial marijuana production is rural. Clandestine labs for producing methamphetamines and designer drugs are also commonly set up in rural areas, where strong fumes are less likely to be detected. Rural areas are often key transshipment points for drugs: rural highway interdictions have led to large seizures, safe houses for storing smuggled drugs are often set up in rural areas, and smugglers take advantage of the many isolated air strips set up for corporate farms.

Rural areas generally have much lower arrest rates, perhaps by as much as a factor of four. Greater informal control and closer social networks may serve to limit or suppress the misbehavior and criminality that often accompany drug use, and they may also encourage police to deal with minor drug violators informally. Rural police usually have fewer resources, including less manpower and less support, which may restrict their ability to respond proactively to drug-related problems. These features of the rural environment present special problems that cannot be addressed by urban solutions.

Policy recommendations

- **Community-specific policies.** Wide variations among rural communities (e.g., in wealth, geographic isolation, or population density) in different parts of the U.S. raise questions about the wisdom of developing blanket national policies for uniform application.

- **Prevention programs.** Although research has correctly questioned the effectiveness of existing prevention programs, they should be continued in rural areas, at least in the short run. No alternative programs exist that are demonstrably superior in preventing youth drug use, and the public demands that some action be taken against the problem. The programs also improve communication between schools, police, and students in rural areas. In the long run, programs like Drug Abuse Resistance Education (D.A.R.E.), which build bridges between the police and schools, might be modified to include other groups, such as treatment centers, civic organizations, and churches. Prevention programs should capitalize on and reinforce the closer ties among individuals and groups that characterize many rural communities.

- **Reduced Federal presence.** Policies that require direct Federal involvement in enforcement should be approached with caution. Rural citizens and police often view Federal authorities with suspicion, and Federal authorities are often not fully aware of the nuances of the local culture. More promising approaches are those that facilitate cooperative efforts between local and Federal authorities, or those in which Federal authorities serve to support locally directed actions.

■ **Rural task forces.** Short-term actions should include continued Federal support for rural task forces, which have proven valuable as a way to combine the expertise and knowledge of the local police with the technical skills and resources of other local police, State police, and Federal authorities. Task forces may also provide an avenue for facilitating improved relations between rural (i.e., local) police and both State and Federal authorities. An examination should be made of why small departments are not more actively involved in task forces, since their size and budgets would make participation especially valuable.

■ **Resource sharing.** Resource sharing among police agencies in rural areas and between rural agencies and others at the State and Federal levels should be facilitated, in the short term. Assistance in locating special equipment would enhance rural drug enforcement efforts; as a long-term measure, an office to provide this help should be established.

■ **Training.** In 1994, the State and Local Training Division of the Federal Law Enforcement Training Center (FLETC) used input from rural police to develop a training program for rural drug enforcement. The program's content is excellent, but getting the training to rural police is extremely difficult because of cost and a shortage of officers to provide shift coverage for those who leave for training. FLETC's "train the trainer" approach to rural drug enforcement training is probably the best that can be done at present.

■ **Training delivery.** However, a system is needed for more directly taking training to rural areas. One option is to utilize the extensive network of community colleges found in many States. Community colleges are linked through electronic networks, making it possible to send training out to relatively remote areas from a central location. The Federal Government could provide assistance in resolving the technical issues of delivery, and FLETC could play an important role in helping States develop, implement, and update training tailored to the unique rural circumstances of each State.

DRUGS AND THE URBAN COMMUNITY

Issues

Involvement in the illicit drug underclass has a wide-ranging negative impact on inner-city neighborhoods. The subculture demonstrates a set of values, beliefs, lifestyles, and behavioral norms that devalue legitimate means of earning money and embrace self-serving manipulation, the "fast life," and the use of violence. With the emergence of crack, the more stable organized crime groups that had been responsible for the distribution of heroin and cocaine gave way to independent, low-level crack sellers. Driven by high profits, crack distribution escalated in neighborhoods that experienced social and economic deprivation. Within these inner-city neighborhoods, crack distribution networks operate in a fluid market economy that allows freelance crack distributors to sell crack with minimal investment capital, street sellers to switch suppliers easily and control their own work schedules, and violence to flourish as a growing army of young urban crack sellers compete to protect their economic interests.

Law enforcement efforts to reduce drug use have been directed at identifying and convicting those individuals at the top of the vertical hierarchy of major drug distribution groups, in the belief that such a strategy would make it more difficult for consumers to locate drugs of choice. Thus, prices would increase, and consumption would be driven downward. Police crackdowns, whether sweeping or focused, are an alternative strategy aimed at making it more difficult to carry out drug transactions and frustrating participants at all levels of the drug distribution system. However, available research shows that the extent of drug trafficking and the crime, violence, and lawlessness associated with drugs in the inner cities have not diminished despite increasingly punitive local, State, and Federal Government interventions and social control. On the contrary, these social troubles have increased, in the midst of an ever-escalating and costly "war on drugs."

Summary

For the most part, inner-city communities house many African-American and Hispanic residents whose populations have been replenished (since the flight of middle-class professional and working-class blacks from ghetto communities) by poorer, younger newcomers from rural areas. These late arrivals were born at a time when structural shifts in the economy resulted in the relocation of manufacturing industries outside the central city, a bifurcation into high- and low-wage income sectors, and dramatic technological innovation. These shifts, coupled with the exodus of those who provided stability and helped to reinforce societal values and norms, have caused inner-city communities to experience increased joblessness and a decline in basic institutions that have led to social disorganization.

Policy recommendations

■ **Economic and social context.** Drug research, and the policy stemming from it, should account for the connection between the economic and social environments into which many drug users are born. Drug use and drug addiction are tied to structural conditions that help to create a self-perpetuating cycle of pathology, which must be viewed and addressed holistically.

■ **Community-based programs.** Drug and crime intervention should concentrate on chronic heroin, cocaine, and injection drug users. Arrest brings many users into contact with the criminal justice system; this contact should be used to detect and assess drug use and present treatment options. Arrestees who test positive for substance abuse should be placed in treatment while detained. Therefore, community-based sentencing and intervention programs should be considered, rather than jail or prison, for drug abuse/possession charges.

■ **Mandatory treatment.** Chronic abusers who are sentenced to jail or prison should be compelled to enroll in treatment programs. Once these offenders have been released on probation or parole, legal supervision should be lengthy to reduce the likelihood of recidivism, and community-based treatment should be required.

■ **Treatment evaluation.** To determine treatment needs, an evaluation of the extent of criminal involvement should be made; research indicates that the longer an individual remains in a treatment program, the greater the continuity of care, and the greater the likelihood of successful employment and reduced drug- and crime-related activities.

■ **Media and school strategies.** Although gains have been made through the use of mass media campaigns, informational lectures, and denouncements made by celebrity role models, drug prevention programs must recognize that young people are impulsive, have undeveloped self-esteem, have peer-centered lives, and are easily seduced by the streets and the promise of quick and easy money. In some inner-city school settings, "resistance skills training" teaches students how to recognize and cope with peer pressure, thereby improving their social competency.

Additional evaluated experimental projects should be conducted to determine the effectiveness of this psychosocial strategy designed to discourage drug use.

■ **Geographically focused enforcement.** Community-based surveys of drug locations should be conducted to identify the nature of drug markets and the way that abusers utilize them. Once identified, the activity of drug markets can be investigated in terms of the convergence of consumers and sellers in space and time. In this way, it would be possible to realistically depict the drug distribution patterns in urban areas and identify specific places of ongoing drug activity for intervention.

■ **Root cause strategy.** Consideration should be given to a drug strategy aimed at ameliorating those conditions that give rise to drug use in the inner city, namely, a strategy that emphasizes education, job training, psychological support systems, and drug prevention. Joblessness is a fundamental problem that must be addressed, and assistance with child support programs, child care strategies, family allowance programs, and parenting skills training is needed to improve the overall life chances of children.

DRUGS AND THE COMMUNITY

Public perception, scholarly research, and public policy often equate the drug problem with urban problems. Similarly, an erroneous nexus between citizens of color and the U.S. drug problem is frequently made by average Americans, politicians, and government officials. An examination of the most recent *Uniform Crime Reports* indicates, however, that among suburban arrestees for drug abuse violations in 1993, 71.5 percent were white, while the comparable white proportion of rural arrestees for such offenses was 75.9 percent. In contrast, whites made up 56 percent of city arrestees for drug abuse violations in 1993.

Knowledge about suburban and rural drug issues is sparse, but the available evidence suggests that drugs are a serious concern in rural areas. Many rural drug problems are identical to those in urban communities. It also appears that unique features of the rural environment present special problems that cannot be solved by urban solutions. Further, urban and rural areas feed each other's drug problems. Drugs flow from cities into the countryside, but they also flow from the countryside into cities. Thus, this discussion is focused on drugs in rural and urban communities.

Findings of Existing Research

The Rural Community

There is a tremendous volume of research on illicit drug issues, but only a very small portion of that research includes rural communities. The existing research on rural drug problems is particularly interesting considering that rural communities have substantially lower rates of crime, including violent crime, than urban areas.

Drug use. Most studies that compare rural and urban drug use rates are based on adolescent samples. In general, rural and urban youths are equally likely to be drug users, but there are some differences in the types of drugs used. Cocaine and crack-cocaine use is generally lower in rural areas, but the use of inhalants and stimulants is higher than in urban areas. The press has suggested that such drugs as crack are making their way into rural areas, but it is still too early to verify that this happens with enough frequency to be of special concern.

Evidence is only circumstantial, but it is likely that the link between drug use and violence is weaker in rural areas than in cities. While urban and rural rates of drug use are similar, rural areas have substantially less violent crime—except for domestic violence, for which urban and rural rates are about equal. Teachers and students in rural schools report similar or even greater drug problems in their schools than teachers and students in urban schools, but in rural schools they consistently report less violence.

Finally, while the rates of illegal drug use may be comparable across urban and rural areas, data from a variety of sources suggest that alcohol use is a much greater problem in rural areas. The greater use of alcohol, combined with the distances to be traveled and the lack of public transportation, also mean that driving under the influence (DUI) is a serious rural problem, with the arrest rate about double that in urban areas.

Drug production, trafficking, and transshipment. Drugs are not only consumed in rural areas, they are often produced there. It is estimated that 25–50 percent of the marijuana consumed in the United States is domestically grown. While it is possible to set up large marijuana cultivation sites in urban areas, nearly all commercial marijuana production is rural, and this is likely to be true for some years to come. Clandestine laboratories for producing methamphetamines and designer drugs are also commonly set up in rural areas, where strong fumes are less likely to be detected.

Little is known about drug trafficking in rural areas, or about the nature and extent of networks between urban and rural traffickers. Some networks, however loose, must exist to allow the movement of drugs between rural and urban areas (e.g., moving domestic marijuana into urban areas and cocaine into rural areas). There are some reports of urban gangs using major highways to move drugs into small towns around larger cities, but this routing probably accounts for a small proportion of the drugs moved into and out of rural areas.

Finally, rural areas are often key transshipment points for drugs. Rural highway interdictions have led to large seizures, safe houses for storing smuggled drugs are often set up in rural areas, and smugglers take advantage of the many isolated airstrips set up for corporate farms.

Drug enforcement. The use of drugs may be at comparable levels in urban and rural communities, but rural areas generally have much lower arrest rates, perhaps by as much as a factor of four. There are several possible reasons for this. First, the greater informal control and closer social networks may serve to limit or suppress the misbehavior and criminality that often accompany drug use. These same social forces may encourage police to more frequently deal with minor drug violators informally. A second factor that may account for lower drug arrest rates in rural areas is that rural police generally have fewer resources, including less manpower and less support. Some have argued that drug arrest rates depend heavily on how proactively police pursue drug cases. Limited manpower and support may restrict the ability of rural police to respond proactively regarding drugs.

Whatever the reason for the low drug arrest rates in rural areas, it is *not* because rural police are indifferent to the drug problem. To the contrary, it is a major concern. A recent survey of rural sheriffs and small-town police chiefs asked them to prioritize their concerns from a list of 22 issues. Drug issues were ranked number one, followed closely by domestic violence. All other issues trailed far behind.

The Urban Community

Drug use and the inner city. While inner-city communities continued experiencing growing rates of poverty, increased social disorganization, and escalating rates of violent and property crime, a new smokable form of cocaine emerged on the streets of American cities. Crack gained both media and

political attention. Early reports from users suggested that once initiated, compulsive crack use often followed. Consequently, all manner of social problems were ascribed to crack's meteoric rise.

Researchers continued to focus their attention on the alleged link between drug use and criminal activity. While some maintained a connection, others asserted that the drug-crime hypothesis was only correlational in nature—that crime preceded the use of illicit drugs—or that the association was the result of shared antecedents, such as family background, peer association and influences, and social class. Whatever the association, researchers argue that involvement in the drug and criminal underclass has a wide-ranging, negative impact on inner-city neighborhoods.

The criminal drug subculture demonstrates a set of values, beliefs, lifestyles, and conduct norms that appear to embrace devaluation of legitimate means to earn money, manipulation for the offender's benefit, adherence to the use of illicit income to support the "fast life," and the use of violence to support the offender's reputation. These focal concerns of large numbers of drug-addicted offenders contribute to the continued decline of inner-city communities.

Inner-city drug trafficking. Historically, the drug distribution research literature has focused on heroin. The importance of Jews and Italians in the systematic importation and sale of heroin in New York City, and the lower levels of the heroin distribution system have been described. Cocaine selling was less common prior to 1970; however, it was noted that the organizational structure of cocaine sellers was similar to that of heroin sellers and that, by 1976, cocaine sellers outnumbered heroin sellers in New York City by 2 to 1. While this ratio is generally still the case, the current resurgence of heroin, particularly in purer forms than were prevalent in the 1970's, suggests parallel drug threats.

With the emergence of crack, the more stable, organized crime groups, which had been responsible for the distribution of heroin, gave way to independent crack sellers who participated in low-level, street-selling activities. Driven by high profits, crack distribution escalated in neighborhoods that experienced social and economic deprivation. Within these inner-city neighborhoods, crack distribution networks consisted of a dynamic system of entry-level positions that operated in a rather fluid market economy that allowed freelance crack distributors to sell crack with minimal investment capital. As a result of the low skill levels and minimal initial resource outlay required to sell crack, as well as the competition for buyers, systemic violence flourished as a growing army of young, inner-city crack sellers attempted to protect their economic interests.

The structure of dealing organizations has been described as a social system consisting of traffickers, dealers, sellers, and low-level distributors. The ability of street sellers to switch to several different suppliers and to control their work schedules underscores the fluidity of the drug distribution system in inner-city communities.

Research studies have documented crack use and distribution in New York City, Miami, Detroit, Los Angeles, and Philadelphia. In Detroit, most crack purchases occur primarily indoors, and crack houses are the principal retailing outlets for crack. While crack houses are distribution sites in Detroit, most crack sales occur on street corners in Philadelphia. These studies demonstrate that the explosion of crack has reconfigured the economics of selling drugs and has resulted in the establishment of vertically controlled selling organizations. As market demands increase, competition becomes a driving force in this organizational system.

Drug enforcement. This structure and the variety of roles performed by members of the inner-city illegal drug organizations serve to reduce the effectiveness of law enforcement agents in their attempts to arrest sellers. Law enforcement efforts to reduce drug use have been directed at identifying and convicting those individuals at the top of the vertical hierarchy of major drug distribution groups. It is believed that such a strategy will make it more difficult for consumers to locate their drugs of choice; therefore, prices will increase and consumption will be driven downward.

An alternative strategy—sweeping the streets—involves making arrests based on actual police observations. This strategy requires the substantial presence of both uniformed and undercover officers in drug distribution sites and changing the environmental conditions of drug hot spots (such as street lighting

conditions). However, these types of sweeps yield more arrests than can be processed by either the police or other components of the criminal justice system. The idea of a focused police crackdown in cities with large drug problems avoids some of the problems inherent in the indiscrete drug sweep. These strategies are aimed at making it more difficult to carry out drug transactions and to frustrate participants at all levels of the drug distribution system. Unfortunately, inner-city minorities bear the brunt of such escalated criminal justice activity.

The Policy Relevance of Existing Research

Rural Considerations

Understanding the policy relevance of existing research first requires understanding rural settings, particularly those features that distinguish rural and urban communities. Two of these features are social: a reliance on informal control and a mistrust of government, particularly a strong centralized government. Rural citizens change addresses less frequently and are more likely than their urban counterparts to personally know others in the community. This often sets the stage for solving problems informally, including minor crime problems. In addition to this reliance on informal control, and perhaps a logical extension of it, is the fact that rural citizens are more likely to mistrust a strong centralized government and the programs associated with it.

It must also be appreciated that the social meaning of something is not always the same in urban and rural areas. For example, gun ownership is much more common in rural areas, but the percentage of crimes that are committed with guns is lower in rural areas. Guns clearly have a different meaning for rural citizens, and drug policies that include the issue of guns should take this into account.

In addition to these social factors, constructing policies related to drugs in rural areas requires appreciating the problems that arise from geographic size, physical isolation, and a small and often widely dispersed population. Further, some of the deepest pockets of poverty are in rural areas. This poverty provides an incentive—or at least a rationalization—for entering into the drug business. Poverty also means a small tax base for locally funded prevention, treatment, and enforcement programs.

Finally, policies must be able to deal with the wide variations across rural areas. Describing the "average" rural community is important, but generic depictions may gloss over crucial variations across rural areas. For example, while the average rural county has a high poverty level, some are quite wealthy. And, while geographic isolation is a serious issue in such States as Arizona or Montana, it is at most a minor issue in "rural" Delaware or Maryland.

What we know about drugs in rural areas has several implications for policy. Drug use is not exclusively an urban phenomenon; rural citizens are not simply consumers of drugs but are also drug producers and are affected by the flow of drugs through their communities. It is clear that there is a very real foundation for the concerns of rural citizens about drugs in their communities and that their concerns are shared by rural police. Thus, ignoring rural drug problems is to ignore genuine concerns of rural citizens and their police. At the same time, policies that require direct Federal involvement in enforcement should be approached with caution. Rural citizens and rural police often view Federal authorities with suspicion, and Federal authorities are often not fully aware of the nuances of the local rural culture. More promising approaches are those that facilitate cooperative efforts between local and Federal authorities, or those in which Federal authorities serve to support locally directed actions.

The likelihood that violence is less frequently linked to drugs in rural areas suggests caution so that policies are not adopted that increase the likelihood of violence while also generating public hostility against authorities. Recognizing the rural drug problem and an enthusiasm for eradicating drugs should not turn rural communities into war zones.

In sum, the unique features of the rural setting raise questions about the wisdom of simply applying urban solutions to rural drug problems. The rural-urban differences are too great for this to be successful. Additionally, the wide variations among rural communities in different parts of the United States raise questions about the wisdom of developing blanket national

policies that are applied in the same way to all rural areas. The variations among rural areas are too great for a single broad solution.

Urban Considerations

It is clear that the "War on Drugs" first launched under the Nixon administration a quarter of a century ago and disproportionately targeted at U.S. inner-city racial and ethnic minorities has been a dismal failure. Available research reveals that the extent of drug trafficking and the crime, violence, and lawlessness associated with drugs in the inner cities of this Nation have not diminished despite increasingly punitive Federal, State, and local interventions and social control. On the contrary, such social ills have increased despite an ever-escalating and costly war.

To some, social problems in the United States are centered exclusively in the Nation's urban centers. Researchers and the general public view inner-city communities as areas most affected by a tangle of pathology that produces all sorts of social ills. In this context, drug use becomes a symptom of the relative decline of inner-city communities.

For the most part, inner-city communities are the places of residence for many African Americans and Hispanics. Further, these populations have been replenished by the migration of poor newcomers from rural areas that has skewed the age profiles of these communities. These populations tend to be younger than their white counterparts. Researchers demonstrate that the higher the group's median age, the higher the group's income, while the lower the group's median age, the higher the group's unemployment rate and crime rate. It is important to remember that the population explosion among minority youths occurred at a time when structural shifts occurred in the economy. These structural shifts resulted in the relocation of manufacturing industries to locations outside the central city, the bifurcation of the low-wage and high-wage sectors of the economy, and innovation in technology. In turn, these factors resulted in increased joblessness for this segment of the population. In addition to growing joblessness, increasing numbers of middle-class professional and working-class African Americans no longer reside in or service ghetto communities. Middle-class professional and working-class African Americans had provided stability to inner-city neighborhoods and had helped to reinforce societal norms and values. Therefore, the removal of these families from the inner city has made it difficult to sustain the basic institutions of life in these communities. The decline in the basic institutions has also meant a corresponding decline in social organization in the inner city.

Analysts have all too often studied drug addiction in isolation from racial inequality, teenage pregnancy, female-headed families, welfare dependency, and other social dislocations experienced by those who are members of the growing urban underclass. Drug use research has not addressed the connections between the economic and social environments into which many drug users are born. Drug use and drug addiction have not been tied to the structural conditions that help to create a self-perpetuating cycle of pathology.

Recommendations for Action

It is usually easier to describe what is, than to speak with certainty about what policies should be. In addition, the limited research on drugs in rural communities provides less background information for developing policy than is true in urban areas. With these provisos in mind, there are several courses of action that would seem to be justified by the existing research.

Drug prevention and drug treatment. Drug prevention appears to be well received in rural areas. The studies of urban and rural students mentioned above showed that drugs were equally available in both settings. These same studies also found that rural students were more likely to report taking part in drug treatment programs. Research suggests that rural police are very strongly committed to programs such as Drug Abuse Resistance Education (D.A.R.E.) and see themselves as playing a valuable role in delivering drug prevention to local youth.

Given that urban and rural communities have comparable levels of drug use and that alcohol use is more frequent in rural areas, it is obvious that the treatment needs of rural communities are substantial. Drug treatment in a rural environment is a two-edged sword. On the one hand, the close personal networks and higher levels of informal control may facilitate treatment. This has been observed in a rural commu-

nity that has a large population of addicts from a nearby city who are staying in "sobriety houses" in the community. At the same time, drug treatment is complicated in rural areas by the physical distances that must often be traveled to reach treatment and by the diseconomies of scale that accompany providing services to a widely scattered population. Treatment providers in rural areas are more likely to rely on outpatient services and on such outreach programs as hot lines and crisis intervention. Treatment is also sometimes complicated, and sometimes helped, by the difficulty of maintaining patient confidentiality in small, socially closed communities.

There is substantial evidence that drug treatment programs are effective if the patients remain in them. Therefore, *retention* appears to be the most important factor in determining success. Evidence suggests that individuals who enter community-based treatment programs as a condition of parole or probation— when those conditions are effectively monitored and enforced—tend to stay in programs longer than individuals who enter programs without such compulsion. Civil commitment involves sending drug users to residential treatment centers and then, as a condition of their release back into the community, requiring the users to enroll in an outpatient program in which their drug use is monitored and they are supplied with a variety of supportive services. The key to civil commitment appears to be supervision and enforcement.

Chronic drug-using offenders. Within urban areas, drug and crime intervention should concentrate on chronic heroin, cocaine, and injection drug users. Since many users have contact with the criminal justice system through arrest, this contact should be used to detect and assess any drug use and to present treatment options. Those arrestees who test positive for substance use should be placed in treatment while they are detained. Therefore, when possible, community-based sentencing and intervention programs should be considered rather than jail or prison for drug abuse and drug possession charges.

Chronic abusers who are sentenced to jail or prison should be compelled to enroll in treatment programs. Significant research indicates that correction-based treatment can have a substantial impact. Once these offenders have been released on probation or parole, legal supervision should be lengthy to reduce the likelihood of relapsing. During this period of legal supervision, probationers and parolees should be enrolled in community-based treatment programs. The research indicates that the longer an individual remains in a treatment program, the greater the continuity of care and the greater the likelihood of successful employment and a reduction in drug- and crime-related activities. Consequently, it is important to estimate the extent to which the criminal population is criminally involved in order to determine treatment needs.

Drug prevention. Drug prevention programs such as D.A.R.E. seem especially popular in rural communities, with police as well as citizens. Research has correctly questioned the effectiveness of D.A.R.E. in preventing youth drug use. However, there are three reasons why such programs should be continued, at least in the short run. First, there are no alternative programs that are demonstrably superior in preventing youth drug use. And, given the history of substance abuse prevention programs in general, no such alternative should be expected soon. A second reason for maintaining such programs is that they seem to be very popular in rural areas. Without viable alternative programs to respond to the public's demand that something be done about youthful drug use, leaving a vacuum seems unnecessary and unwise. The third reason for keeping programs such as D.A.R.E. is that they appear to serve the useful function of improving communication among schools, police, and students in rural areas. There are no systematic data to prove this, but it is consistent with other observations about rural communities and rural police, and it is consistent with the beliefs of many rural police.

In the long run, such programs as D.A.R.E., which build bridges between the police and the schools, might be modified to include other groups, such as treatment centers, civic organizations, and churches. That is, prevention programs should capitalize on and reinforce the closer ties among individuals and groups that characterize many rural communities.

Some prevention efforts have been based on the assumption that drug users are ignorant of the deleterious effects of drug use and that when made aware of these effects, they will cease using drugs. While it is true that much has been gained by the use of mass media campaigns, informational lectures, and the use of celebrities as role models to condemn the use of drugs, prevention programs must recognize that young people are impulsive, have undeveloped self-esteem, have peer-centered lives, and are easily seduced by the streets and the "fast" life. In some inner-city school settings "resistance skills training" teaches students how to recognize and cope with peer pressure, thereby improving the social competency of students. Additional evaluated experimental projects should be conducted in order to determine the effectiveness of this psychosocial strategy designed to discourage drug use.

Drug enforcement. Regarding drug enforcement, short-term actions should include continued support for rural task forces. These have proven valuable as a way to combine the expertise and knowledge of the local police with the technical skills and resources of other local police, State police, and Federal authorities. Statistically, rural agencies have been less likely than urban agencies to take part in task forces. This is ironic since their small size and limited resources may make task force participation particularly beneficial. Task forces may also provide an avenue for facilitating improved relations between rural (i.e., local) police and both State and Federal authorities. Federal support for task forces should continue, and there should be an examination of why small departments are not more actively involved in them.

Resource sharing. Another short-term action is to facilitate resource sharing among police agencies in rural areas and between rural agencies and others at the State and Federal levels. Small departments occasionally need special equipment for drug investigations, but this need may be infrequent, perhaps even a one-time event. In these circumstances buying the equipment may not make good economic sense. Even when the expenditure can be justified, a small department may not be able to afford the cost. Assistance in locating special equipment would enhance rural drug enforcement efforts. Long-term actions might include establishing an office to assist local agencies in their searches. This office would not directly distribute equipment but would help agencies to locate the specific equipment that they need.

Training. Finally, there is the issue of training for rural drug enforcement. In 1994 the State and Local Training Division of the Federal Law Enforcement Training Center (FLETC) used input from rural police to develop a training program for rural drug enforcement. The content of the program is excellent, but getting the training to rural police is extremely difficult. Where departments are very small—fewer than 10 officers—there is a high interest in training. However, the expense is often problematic for very small departments. Perhaps a greater problem is that leaving the area for even a week can put excessive demands on the remaining officers and may leave shifts without coverage. FLETC has adopted a "train the trainer" approach to rural drug enforcement training, and this is probably the best that can be done in the short term.

Over the long term there needs to be a system for more directly taking training to rural areas. The precise manner in which this can be done is unclear, but one promising option is to utilize the extensive network of community colleges found in many States. In many States community colleges are linked through electronic networks, making it possible to send training out to relatively remote areas from a central location. The Federal Government could provide assistance in resolving the technical issues of delivery, and FLETC could play an important role in helping States develop, implement, and update training tailored to the unique rural circumstances of each State.

Identification of drug markets. Each year police departments in urban areas establish strike forces and develop strategies for combating crime on the streets. However, most of these strategies have been developed without any understanding of the nature of drug markets and the manner by which abusers utilize these markets. The identification of these markets should involve community-based surveys of drug locations. Once identified, the activity of drug markets can be investigated in terms of the convergence of consumers and sellers in space and time. In this way, it would be possible to realistically depict the drug distribution patterns in urban areas and to identify specific places of ongoing drug activity for intervention. Therefore, such a strategy might reveal that drug activity is confined to specific areas of the city and that markets differ in terms of their intensity, size, and social character. Consequently, enforcement strategies should be geographically focused.

Police drug crackdowns. Once the dimensions and characteristics of drug hot spots have been identified, police drug crackdowns have been one strategy directed at these urban areas. Police drug crackdowns have sought to reduce the visibility of drug transactions, the amount of drugs consumed, the size of the drug-using population, and the street crime associated with drug use and drug trafficking. It has also been reasoned that police drug crackdowns directly affect the quality of life in a community because citizens are reassured and are less fearful. Police crackdowns enhance residents' confidence in law enforcement. However, the question remains as to whether normal enforcement efforts can enhance the offender's perceived risk or likelihood of apprehension.

Research. As to long-term prospects in the urban arena, we find that the majority of social science studies of drug users illustrate social deviance, and addiction is portrayed as a total way of life. Therefore, attention has been directed to remedy the deviant actor, and the conceptual models found in the core of the early drug literature were either criminal models or medical models. Newer studies, however, adopt a view that suggests that addicts are "victims." Nonetheless, the portrayal of addicts as deviants persists since causality resides within some constellation of the family, community, or culture of the addict. Consequently, studies make few connections to any larger social, political, and economic contexts.

The debate over drug legalization continues to occupy the research agendas of countless scholars. Central in this debate is the question of whether the costs associated with drug use are higher if drugs are legalized. Illegal drug use results in increased law enforcement costs, welfare costs, and moral costs. Legalizing drugs results in the possible unknown costs associated with an increase in drug consumption. The predominant drug strategy has focused on increasing the price, difficulty, and inconvenience associated with obtaining drugs, as well as relying on the risks associated with consumption of a product of unknown quality. Virtually little concern has been given to a drug strategy aimed at ameliorating those conditions that continue to give rise to drug use in the inner city: namely, an effective strategy for the inner city that emphasizes education, job training, psychosocial support systems, and drug prevention.

Conclusion

Although they have been relatively ignored in research and policy, illegal drugs are an issue in rural America and are considered among the most pressing problems facing rural police. These rural drug issues include consumption, production, and transshipment. A variety of issues, including geography, economics, low population density, and rural culture, shape the rural drug problem and the strategies for responding to it. For both practical and philosophical reasons there are limits on the extent to which the Federal Government should become more directly involved in rural drug enforcement. However, there are a variety of ways in which the Federal Government can support and enhance local anti-drug efforts in both drug abuse prevention and drug law enforcement.

The value of work and joblessness are fundamental problems that must be addressed. The ideal solution would be to develop a combination of macroeconomic policy, job training programs, and labor market strategies. However, these universalist strategies must also include exceptional programs that will provide income support to lift all families out of poverty. Concurrently, a recognition of policies to promote balanced economic growth must coexist with those strategies designed to improve the overall life chances of children by providing child support programs, child care strategies, family allowance programs, and programs designed to improve parenting skills.

Violence Against Women: Overview

RAPE AND THE CRIMINAL JUSTICE SYSTEM

Summary

Issues

As a result of a nation-wide, grassroots effort made during the past 20 years to reform rape laws in this country, each of the 50 States has in some way modified its traditional rape statutes. These reforms encompassed three goals: to treat rape like any other crime by concentrating on the unlawful acts of the offender, to encourage victims to come forward about rape, and to facilitate the successful prosecution and conviction of rapists. However, research has shown that reforms have fallen far short of achieving their goals: The incidence and prevalence of rape have not significantly declined; reporting has not dramatically risen; and the rates of arrest, prosecution, and conviction of rapists have not appreciably improved.

Similarly, findings show that corroboration requirements persist in a de facto manner, resistance standards continue to provide the basis for decisionmaking, and past sexual activity evidence still influences the treatment of rape cases—in spite of enactment of shield legislation. Moreover, victim credibility remains an issue for courtroom participants (as well as for the public) and all too often accompanies beliefs about victim culpability. Attributions that blame victims perpetuate the persecution of rape victims, rather than the successful prosecution of rape offenders.

Policy considerations and recommendations

- **Marital rape.** Some States still do not legally recognize marital rape, while others have extended this exemption to cohabitors. Legal initiatives are needed on this issue.

- **Victim anonymity.** One particularly difficult issue that demands redress is protection of the anonymity of victims who pursue prosecution. Laws and policies that forbid disclosure of victims' names and addresses are important for victim privacy; however, First Amendment considerations, as well as concerns that perpetuation of the rape stigma results from anonymity protection, have both arisen.

- **Accountability.** Discretionary decisionmaking must be made more visible and criminal justice officials held more accountable for the decisions that shape the implementation of reforms. Implementation should be monitored, incentives should be created, and public pressure should be used to achieve compliance.

- **Victim compensation.** Recourse for victims (for the costs and pains of victimization, such as lost work days, medical bills, etc.) should be expanded through the development of new programs (that do not exclude large categories of victims, such as violent crime victims). Compensation programs need to be funded and extended at all levels of government.

- **Victim advocacy.** For victim advocacy to begin to meet the overwhelming need for services, financial support for rape crisis centers and victim-witness units must grow. Local programs could productively network with national political action committees (PAC's) and organizations, such as the National Organization for Women or the League of Women Voters, to mobilize resources.

- **Outreach to minorities.** Racial and ethnic minorities are underserved. Outreach efforts, such as providing multilingual services, hiring minority staff, forging links with existing community services, and providing community education, should be expanded.

■ **Training for information providers.** In order to make the criminal justice system as non-threatening to victims as possible, it is important to continue providing special training for criminal justice personnel, including police, prosecutors, and judges. Multidisciplinary teams consisting of criminal justice professionals and sexual assault counselors should provide such training. Similarly, dedicated units/personnel to deal with "sex crimes" should be continued.

■ **Public awareness.** Media campaigns are needed to help make rape a national priority and place it on an agenda for change. Media slogans have been effective in combating other social problems and could be developed for rape issues. Similarly, films could be rated for degrees of sexism and the derogation of women, with particular emphasis on how violence against women is portrayed. Another possible model for intervention is the town meeting; town meetings with criminal justice personnel, educators, academicians, and social services providers could be coordinated as part of a national plan to prioritize the problems of rape and violence against women.

■ **Cultural change.** Systematic education, starting with young people, is needed to challenge the traditional cultural beliefs and values that lead to sexual violence. The approbation of sexist notions, inequalities, and violence contributes to our "rape culture." A vision, plan, or program that ignores sex and power differences addresses only symptoms, not root causes, of violence against women.

■ **Research needs.** Statistics on the incidence and prevalence of rape and sexual assaults need to be improved for accurate measurement of these problems nationwide. Some definitions should be changed to reflect new legal categories, and new data (e.g., on the discretionary decisions rendered in rape cases) should be collected. More extensive research on the implementation of reforms should be funded to point the way for new efforts. More recent reforms, such as Federal Rules 413–415 that make admissible the sexual history of offenders, also need to be examined for their impact on the treatment of rape cases.

WOMEN BATTERING AND THE CRIMINAL JUSTICE SYSTEM

Summary

Issues

Domestic and other forms of violence against women are embedded in wider issues, such as male dominance, sexism, racism, and poverty. Although the ultimate prevention of violence against women entails cultural change—e.g., debunking the belief in violence, including corporal punishment, as an effective or acceptable means of social control—victims cannot wait for cultural change.

There have been significant changes in the criminal justice definition of, and response to, domestic violence in the past 20 years, but these changes have not always resulted in greater protection for women who are violently assaulted by their intimate partners. Various studies to measure the deterrent effect of police response in situations where women have been battered by cohabiting intimates have, at best, confused the issue. It seems that arrest, per se, has not uniformly affected the behavior of batterers. Those with greater social bonds or "stakes in conformity" are more likely to be effectively deterred by onscene arrest, while others may be driven to commit more violence.

Mandatory arrest policies may disproportionately affect minority women and those from lower socioeconomic groups, who have fewer resources to settle relationship conflicts by private means. They may face harsher consequences on their household income if the batterer is jailed and may distrust police if racist treatment has characterized prior experiences.

Research supports the view that current police decisionmaking is guided more by speculation and stereotypes than by the wishes and needs of victims, yet it also suggests that the use of criminal law as a resource for women may minimize violence. Police decisions must be guided by the victim's assessment of danger.

Prosecution policy has also been scrutinized for its impact on reducing domestic violence. Findings from the Indianapolis Domestic Violence Prosecution Experiment (IDVPE) suggest that it is not the type of prosecution that is crucial, but that prosecution is initiated. Contrary to popular assumptions, allowing victims who initiated the complaint to drop charges resulted in reducing the risk of further violence. Giving victims this control permits them to use the possibility of abandoning prosecution as a resource in bargaining for their security. Others are empowered by the alliance they form with more powerful others, such as police, prosecutors, and judges. As long as the alliance is steadfast, a victim can threaten to invoke her allies' power to deter her abuser.

Policy recommendations

■ **Victim assessment.** Overall, research indicates that the wishes of the victim are crucial determinants for women's safety in the application of law. Given different circumstances, different women, and different violent men, the victim's assessment of safety and of the impact of applying a criminal sanction must be included in the formula for intervention in domestic violence situations. Given options, including the availability of housing, jobs, and child care, women find ways of stopping violence.

■ **Escape from violence.** The Attorney General should issue short papers disseminating the prevailing wisdom to police/prosecutors/judges/other court personnel, and require ongoing feedback, discussions, and training with local shelters that will provide the locally based examples of good and bad practices with regard to women's attempts to escape violence. Women should not, for example, have to choose between being battered and being homeless, a choice made by more than 50 percent of currently homeless women.

- **Women's shelters.** Shelters should be treated as key components in crime reduction policies. They should be adequately funded and play a central role in any multiagency, community-based strategy. Shelters, and their advice lines, offer crucial services to those most in need—victims of repeated violence—that may assist in reducing further attacks.

- **Education against violence.** The Attorney General should work cooperatively with other concerned Federal agencies to develop an educational program addressing issues such as gender, power, aggression, and competitiveness that are the basis of violence, especially that within the home. This program should become a mandatory element of the school curriculum.

- **Family violence.** The Attorney General should reassemble a Task Force on Family Violence to review where we stand relative to 1984, address new issues that were anticipated by the previous task force, and reassess our needs for research today.

- **Women in prison.** A Federal Task Force on Women in Prison should be established to provide national leadership on the specific plight of incarcerated women, many of whom serve prison terms for violence because they have tried to avert an attack or defend themselves against repeated violence by family members or intimates. Sexual and physical abuse at home also pushes young women to the street, where they learn to numb their pain by using drugs and to survive by petty theft. These women and their children could be better served by nonincarcerative options.

VIOLENCE AGAINST WOMEN:
OVERVIEW

Rape and the Criminal Justice System

Twenty some years after legislative reforms on rape swept across this Nation, the road for progress remains long and arduous. While some progress has been noted in the research literature, the accumulated knowledge is amazingly consistent in demonstrating that rape reforms have fallen far short of achieving their goals. A frequent summarization in the research literature is that the impact of rape reforms has been largely symbolic. Antiquated myths surrounding the sexual violence of rape, along with traditional discriminatory legal requirements and standards, tenaciously cling across our society and criminal justice system, operating to prejudice the handling of rape cases and rape victims.

The specific research findings that identify failure of reforms span a large continuum. Overall, research has shown that rape has not significantly declined; that reporting has not dramatically risen; and that arresting, prosecuting, and convicting rapists has not significantly improved, despite reform efforts to facilitate those objectives. Similarly, corroboration requirements have been found to persist in a de facto manner, despite the lack of their de jure existence; resistance standards continue to be relied upon for decision-making; and past sexual activity evidence influences the treatment of rape cases, regardless of even the best "shield" legislation. Moreover, victim credibility remains an issue for legal actors, as well as for the public, and is all too often concomitant with beliefs about victim culpability. Attributes that blame victims perpetuate persecution of rape victims, rather than successful prosecution of rape offenders.

The following measures should be taken to progress against the problems of rape:

■ **Legislative change.** The nature and magnitude of change vary widely across States, necessitating further legal initiatives in many jurisdictions. For example, some States still do not legally recognize marital rape, while others have extended this exception to cohabitors. One particularly difficult issue that demands redress is the anonymity of victims who pursue prosecution. Laws and policies that forbid disclosure of victims' names and addresses are important for victim privacy; however, First Amendment concerns, as well as concerns that anonymity perpetuates rape stigma, have both arisen.

■ **Monitoring criminal justice.** Discretionary decisionmaking must be made more visible, and criminal justice officials must be held more accountable for the decisions that shape the implementation of reforms. We need to monitor implementation and create incentives and public pressure for compliance.

■ **Recourse for victims.** Recourse for victims for the costs and pains of victimization (for example, lost time at work and medical bills) needs to be expanded through the development of new programs that do not exclude large categories of victims (such as violent crime victims). Compensation programs need to be funded and extended at all levels of government.

■ **Fund services.** Rape crisis centers and victim-witness units have been found to be a powerful source of advocacy for victims, yet these programs struggle simply to exist, given the widely based competition for scarce resources. For victim advocacy to begin to meet the overwhelming need for services, financial support must grow. Local programs could quite productively network with national PAC's and organizations, such as the National Organization for Women and the League of Women Voters, to assist in endeavors and mobilize resources.

■ **Outreach to minorities.** Racial and ethnic minorities are underserved by services. Outreach efforts—including multilingual services, minority hiring, linkages with existing community agencies, and community education—are important for providing victims services.

■ **Inservice training.** It is important to continue to provide special training for police, prosecutors, and judges alike. Multidisciplinary teams consisting of criminal justice professionals and sexual assault counselors are preferable for providing such training. Similarly, dedicated units or personnel to deal with "sex crimes" need to be continued.

■ **Victim information.** All personnel, be they social service, medical, or criminal justice, who come into contact with rape victims need to be knowledgeable about victims' rights, processes, and available services. These same people should be required to inform victims of their rights and tell them what to expect from the legal community and where they can turn for support.

■ **Programs for rape offenders.** Counseling and treatment programs are imperative if the problems of rape are to be truly impacted. Rapists have incredibly high rates of recidivism, indicating that prison alone is ineffective. Rapists must learn that their behavior is not normal and that their actions cannot be rationalized away by victim blaming; it is criminal and heinous behavior.

■ **Data.** Statistics on the incidence and prevalence of rape and sexual assault are problematic. We need to examine and change definitions to reflect new legal categories and, thereby, improve our measurement of rape nationwide (e.g., improve the *Uniform Crime Reports* and the National Crime Survey). Although some changes have been made, data on rape remain problematic. Moreover, new data, such as those on discretionary decisions rendered in rape case processing, need to be collected.

■ **Research.** Much more extensive research on the implementation of reforms needs to be funded to point the way for renewed efforts. This research will serve to identify where and how reforms have failed or succeeded in realizing objectives. More recent reforms such as the Federal Rules 413–415, which make admissible the sexual history of offenders, also need to be examined for their impact on the treatment of rape cases.

■ **Media.** Instead of playing a role in education and prevention, the media perpetuate and aggravate rape and "rape culture." The media could help to make violence against women a national priority on the agenda for change. Media slogans have been shown to be effective tools in combating other social problems and could be developed for rape issues. "Just Say No," for instance, could be adapted and publicized as "No Means No" to garner national attention. Films could be rated for degrees of sexism and the derogation of women, with particular emphasis on how violence against women is portrayed.

■ **Town meetings.** President Clinton's successful engagement of town meetings provides yet another model of possible intervention. Town meetings with criminal justice personnel, educators, academicians, and social service providers could be coordinated as part of a national plan to prioritize the problems of rape and violence against women.

■ **Education and societal attitude change.** We need systematic education, starting with young people, that challenges the traditional cultural beliefs and values leading to sexual violence. A number of innovative programs ranging from elementary school to the university level have shown promise. The approbation of sexist notions of inequality and violence contributes to our "rape culture." The accepting posture toward both the insidious and blatant violence and sexism that permeate this culture serves to lure men to the crimes of sexual as well as nonsexual violence. A vision, plan, or program that ignores sex and power differences will serve only as a Band-Aid, because such measures would address symptoms rather than the root causes of violence against women.

Women Battering and the Criminal Justice System

Violence against women threatens to undermine women's rights to pursue life, liberty, and happiness. Patterns of violence against women reflect a problem of worldwide proportions. Rightly, over the past 20 years, special attention has spotlighted shortcomings in the law, social services, and advice provisions for women facing violence in their homes and elsewhere. As research continues to document, many women imprisoned and hospitalized in the United States have histories that include violence. Finally, domestic and other forms of violence against women must be understood as being embedded in wider issues, such as male dominance, sexism, racism, and poverty.

Sole reliance on the criminal justice system to stop violence against women is a mistaken policy. That said, the failure to set the practice of criminal justice actors into the prevailing wisdom contributes to the danger women face from intimates, former husbands, and others. The police have been the target of much of the research to date. The various studies of police response in situations of cohabiting intimates as a deterrent to men's violence have, at best, confused the issue. It seems that arrest per se did not have a uniform effect on men's behavior; perpetuating the myth that arrest can, in and of itself, deter men's violence is mistaken. Yet, research evidence suggests that the use of criminal law as a resource for women may minimize the violence. Discretionary decisionmaking by the police must be guided by the victim's assessment of danger. All the research supports the view that, at present, police decisionmaking is faulty, guided more by speculation and use of stereotypes than by the wishes and needs of victims, undermining even the best policy within the criminal justice arena.

Prosecution policy has also been scrutinized for its impact on reducing domestic violence. Findings from Ford's study of Indianapolis suggest that it is not the type of prosecution that is crucial, but that prosecution is initiated. Contrary to popular assumptions, allowing victims who initiated the complaint to drop charges resulted in reducing the risk of further violence.

The lessons from police studies and studies focusing on prosecution converge: The wishes of the victim are crucial determinants of women's safety in the application of law. The evidence concurs that, given different circumstances, different women, and different violent men, the victim's assessment of safety and of the impact of a criminal sanction must be included in the formula for intervention in family violence situations. If they have options, which include the availability of housing, jobs, and child care, women find ways of stopping violence. Should they need the assistance of the criminal justice system, the research suggests that it does not often serve their needs.

Recommendations

It is the consensus of the members of this task force that protecting the provisions of the Violence Against Women Act, which provide funds to direct service to women facing violence, is essential for the safety of women. In an era of brutal fiscal cuts to public provision of care, it is also critical to protect the moneys allocated in the recent crime bills for research and encourage creative and innovative practice that is globally informed, yet locally based. The Attorney General can assist this process by disseminating information on flexible, good practice based on experiences of victims, not those of criminal justice personnel.

- **Information dissemination.** The Attorney General should issue short papers that disseminate prevailing wisdom to police, prosecutors, judges, and other court personnel. These papers should require ongoing feedback, discussions, and training with local shelters, which will provide locally based examples of good and bad practice and the methods used by local women to escape violence.

Rationale: Each player in the criminal justice system holds unique personal and institutionally based perspectives on what constitutes justice. Research continually finds patchy adherence to even the best policy; ignorance or disregard about men's violence affects different women differently. Decisionmaking in situations of family violence rarely embraces what women themselves already do to ensure their safety. Women should not, for example, have to choose between being battered and being homeless. We must acknowledge the impact of violence on the criminal justice system: Everyone deals with it but no one takes responsibility. Police should be treated as resources for women and children facing violence. Research indicates that mandating particular ways of responding to calls for assistance does not result in protection. Women should be considered partners in decisions made on their behalf, including decisions to drop charges. Evidence should be gathered that demonstrates how to empower particular victims to manage the violence, with support and backup from statutory and voluntary agencies.

■ **Shelters.** Shelters should be treated as key components in crime reduction policies. They should be funded adequately as key players in any multi-agency, community-based strategy.

Rationale: There is growing acknowledgment among criminologists that crime prevention should be aimed toward those at greatest risk. Victims of repeated violence require continuous support from such resources as police, courts, and hospitals. Shelters and their advice lines offer crucial services to those most in need, which may assist in reducing repeated attacks.

■ **Public education.** The Attorney General should commit U.S. Department of Justice resources in cooperative efforts with other Federal agencies concerned with violence (for example, the National Institute of Justice, together with the Centers for Disease Control and Prevention, an agency within the U.S. Department of Health and Human Services) and prepare an educational program addressing violence (especially within the home) that becomes a mandatory component of the school curriculum. Australia, New Zealand, and Canada have taken such action, which begins to address the foundation of violence by taking seriously the issues of gender, power, aggression, and competitiveness. Public education is also appropriate. One campaign, Zero Tolerance, which took place in Edinburgh, Scotland (and Canada and Australia), featured public posters, television advertisements, advertising during highly popular sporting events (such as soccer and rugby), and local radio coverage, aimed to dispel myths about violence against women.

■ **The Attorney General's Task Force on Family Violence.** The Attorney General should reassemble an Attorney General's Task Force on Family Violence to review where we stand relative to 1984, to address new issues that were anticipated by the previous task force, and to reassess our needs for research today. We nominate Professor Kathleen Ferraro as our representative on this task force.

Rationale: Women and children who face violence are best served by community commitment, demonstrated by links among many agencies, volunteer groups, legal services, hospitals, schools, housing, and emergency help lines. Federal grants should be available to distribute good practice awards to communities demonstrating community responsibility for violence against women and children.

Women and Imprisonment

In the past decade, the number of women in U.S. prisons more than tripled. Sexual abuse and physical violence against women is often correlated with imprisonment. Many women who serve prison terms for violence are incarcerated because they have tried to avert an attack or defend themselves against repeated violence by family members or intimates. Sexual and physical abuse at home also push young women to the street, where they learn to numb their pain by using drugs and survive by resorting to petty theft. These women, whose survival measures are criminalized, increasingly inhabit our prisons. They and their children could be better served by nonincarcerative options. Reduction in women's imprisonment would free an enormous amount of funds to care for them and their children in the community, as well as provide them with necessary resources.

A Federal Task Force on Women in Prison should be established to provide national leadership on the specific needs of women. We propose Professor Meda Chesney-Lind as our representative on this task force.

Editor's note: Members of the Task Force on Violence Against Women also prepared separate reports, listed below, from which this overview distilled findings:

■ "Recommendations for the Task Force on Violence Against Women" by Joanne Belknap (NCJ 158902).

■ "Summarization of Issues and Recommendations on Rape" by Susan Caringella-MacDonald (NCJ 158903).

■ "Women in Prison: Punishing Victims as Penal Policy" by Meda Chesney-Lind (NCJ 158904).

■ "Domestic Violence and the Criminal Justice Response" by Kathleen J. Ferraro (NCJ 158905).

■ "Domestic Violence Against Women" by David A. Ford (NCJ 158906).

■ "Rape: The Impact and Limits of Law Reform" by Julie Horney (NCJ 158907).

■ "Federal Task Force on Violence Against Women" by Susan L. Miller (NCJ 158908).

Copies of these individual reports are available on interlibrary loan or for a photocopy fee.

Contact the National Criminal Justice Reference Service, 1–800–851–3420, and ask for the document by title and NCJ number.

Domestic and International Organized Crime

DOMESTIC ORGANIZED CRIME

Summary

Issues

Although seriously weakened in the past 25 years, the traditional Cosa Nostra form of organized crime has not been eliminated; instead, it has been joined by a variety of increasingly powerful domestic and international organized criminal networks operating in this country. Criminal organizations (particularly those from China and Latin America) are exploiting the increases in U.S. immigration for both cover and concealment of criminal activities, as well as for recruitment. Aliens, smuggled by boat, pay exorbitant passage fees and cannot work at regular jobs; thus, they are exploited by unscrupulous employers or become active in prostitution, the drug trade, or other aspects of the illegal economy. In this way, victims become criminals themselves.

One problem in combating these groups is that citizens have not been mobilized as allies in the effort. Despite a series of significant prosecutions for racketeering conspiracies during the last decade, vast numbers of Americans continue to gamble illegally, use banned drugs, buy stolen property, and otherwise contribute to the very same conspiracies that the government is fighting to defeat.

Policy recommendations

■ **Citizen mobilization.** Special grand jury provisions of the Organized Crime Control Act, calling for an investigative grand jury to be convened at least every 18 months to examine organized crime and corruption in districts of more than one million citizens, should finally be implemented. Significantly, the law provides for the special grand jury to issue a report on those conditions at the end of its term. Implementation would provide a tremendous opportunity for citizens on the grand jury to help educate other citizens, through followup town meetings and other mechanisms, about the less obvious evils of organized crime.

■ **Surveillance.** Specific policy and judicial authorization guidelines should be developed as a way to make installations of eavesdropping and monitoring devices uniform—and the expectations of investigators, their supervisors, and the judiciary identical. There is no way to eliminate the danger of these installations, but law and policy must more specifically circumscribe this issue to protect those in law enforcement and negate the possibility of agency embarrassment, should an incident occur.

■ **Criminal informants.** DOJ should establish a technical assistance program designed to train State and local authorities in the proper development, use, and management of criminal informants, because the misuse of informants has not only misled police but undermined public support for the use of informants. Technical assistance might consist of the development of police courses (required for those handling informants) or inservice training on this issue.

■ **Uniform training standards.** DOJ should develop minimum standards and curriculum for police training nationwide, with special emphasis on the training of local police. Inconsistency in training hurts professionalism, lateral career mobility of officers, and interagency cooperation in combating organized crime.

■ **Seizure of assets.** DOJ should develop specific guidelines for the seizure of assets to set a national standard. Public confidence erodes when seizures are made that appear questionable. Several lawsuits against police are pending on this issue. The incidence or appearance of unprofessional behavior on the part of police in organized crime control efforts must be removed.

- **Tracking illicit drugs.** DOJ should provide incentives and guidelines for States, as well as other nations, to track identified illicit drugs and to prohibit their use under penalty of law. Only 18 States have enacted legislation similar to the Chemical Diversion and Trafficking Act (establishing Federal recordkeeping, reporting, and transaction requirements for essential chemicals), and these laws differ widely in their scope and requirements. Other jurisdictions must also be kept abreast of new synthetic chemicals that should be added each year to the list of essential chemicals.

- **Court-imposed trusteeships.** Court-imposed trusteeships should be utilized against nonunion businesses found to be controlled by organized crime. Such intervention enables the government to "restart" the business with completely new personnel and supervisory and auditing procedures to prevent the return of organized crime. This kind of intercession in nonunion businesses has occurred in few instances thus far, but its potential as a tool for long-term prevention is enormous.

- **Investigative screening.** DOJ should sponsor one or more "teams" of interested researchers and organized crime investigators to work for a period of months, since there has been too little interaction among these professionals. Together, they should test investigative screening models of businesses at high risk of infiltration by organized crime and translate their findings into usable form for investigators at the Federal, State, and local levels. A proven case-screening (or business-screening) model could do much to reduce time spent on proactive investigations that lead to dead ends.

- **Shared perspectives.** DOJ should sponsor "long-term prevention" forums periodically for the specific purpose of integrating law enforcement and criminological perpectives on the problem of organized crime. Expertise and insight on both sides could be profitably shared to develop effective organized crime control innovations.

INTERNATIONAL ORGANIZED CRIME

Summary

Issues

The Federal Government has particular and singular responsibilities with regard to the transnational and international dimensions of organized crime (e.g., international drug trafficking, arms dealing, and murder for hire), which are unique in nature and scope. There is increasing evidence that the wealth and power of criminal organizations in various countries are growing and that international links among these organizations exist. A number of factors associated with this globalization of organized crime have implications for the United States.

A state of ungovernability, instability, and fragmentation in certain countries provides favorable conditions for the development and nurturance of organized criminal groups. This is especially true in the countries that were part of the former Soviet Union, but it also applies to Eastern Europe and countries such as Peru, Burma, Mexico, and Pakistan. These countries provide both operational bases and safe havens for international criminals.

Of continuing special concern is the problem of organized crime operating in and from the former USSR. The so-called "Russian mafia" are operating in Germany, Poland, and virtually every other state in Eastern and Central Europe. There is also a growing problem of organized criminal networks among Soviet emigres in the U.S. In the successor states of the USSR (especially Russia), organized crime is undermining efforts to create the rule of law, as well as attacking various fledgling democratic institutions. Internationally, Russian organized crime's illegal trade in high-tech weaponry, potentially including nuclear weapons, constitutes a considerable threat.

An increasingly sophisticated use of advanced communications technology facilitates the wire transfers of money for laundering on a much greater scale than ever before. The threat to the integrity of international banking is considerable.

Coupled with the amplified scope and magnitude of international organized crime is an inadequate law enforcement response, due to the absence of international cooperation and policy; limited exchange of intelligence and mutual legal assistance; functional and bureaucratic fragmentation among the various criminal justice agencies; a dearth of specialized personnel; competition and turf battles among responsible agencies; and failure to coordinate or harmonize national and international laws.

Policy recommendations

- **Russian racketeering.** The United States should take the lead in helping Russian officials to draft effective anti-racketeering legislation (not necessarily duplicating the Racketeer Influenced and Corrupt Organization (RICO) statute) that is appropriate to and mindful of Russia's special circumstances and legal traditions.

- **Aid tied to reforms.** American and other Western aid to Russia should be specifically targeted to combating organized crime. Steps to be taken in this effort must include reforming the Russian judicial system; equipping law enforcement agencies with vehicles, computers, and other communications equipment; and training and providing technical assistance to law enforcement personnel in organized crime investigative techniques. Consideration should also be given to some kind of salary supplement plan. This aid must be linked to the development of aggressive methods for rooting out (and keeping out) corruption in the criminal justice system.

- **Joint data bank.** A joint Western-Russian data bank on Russian organized crime should be established. This data bank should include the names of individuals and groups known to be involved in organized crime, as well as data on their criminal histories, records of international travel, contacts in the West, criminal enterprises, and legitimate businesses, etc. Interpol might do this or at least play some role in it.

- **Financial Crimes Enforcement Network (FINCEN).** The intelligence-gathering and investigative utility of FINCEN, already demonstrated in areas of international money laundering and banking schemes, and especially those involving Russians, should be expanded.

- **Criminal justice training for Russians.** A broad-based effort to improve the performance of criminal justice officials in the former Soviet Union—through recruitment, training, education, and technical assistance—should be undertaken. This effort should not be limited to include only agencies of the Federal Government, such as the Federal Bureau of Investigation (FBI) and the Drug Enforcement Administration (DEA), but also draw heavily on the resources and valuable expertise at the State and local levels. It should also involve the private sector, e.g., the Police Executive Research Forum, the Police Foundation, the National District Attorneys Association, as well as criminology/criminal justice educators and researchers in colleges and universities.

DEALING WITH DOMESTIC AND INTERNATIONAL ORGANIZED CRIME

In many respects organized crime is unique—different from the subject matter focus of any of the other task forces constituting the National Policy Committee of the American Society of Criminology. Given its nature and scope, it has a potential for harm that is greater than most of these other areas. Organized crime involvement in international drug trafficking, arms dealing, and murder-for-hire are just a few examples supporting this contention. Organized crime has transnational and international dimensions as well as being a domestic concern; it is a crime problem for which the Federal Government has particular and singular responsibilities. These characteristics have important implications for both overall policy and any specific action recommendations.

Coincident with its character, unfortunately, the research and information base for our knowledge of organized crime is extremely weak—weaker than just about any other area of criminological research. Policy recommendations, therefore, can be grounded only partially in good research.

We will briefly outline the limitations of existing research on organized crime and then focus on the policy relevance of what is known. We will conclude by offering a number of policy recommendations for addressing both the domestic and international aspects of organized crime.

What Do We Know About Organized Crime Policy?

Research on organized crime is much more anecdotal and descriptive than research on other forms of crime. There are very few empirical studies—none focusing on global forms of organized crime. Organized crime researchers are very dependent upon documents and reports from law enforcement agencies. These sources, however, are often limited in a variety of ways: by secrecy, by sanitizing of public documents through the production of "disinformation" by certain government agencies, by corruption that distorts reporting, and by the fact that agencies often simply do not know what is happening.

Information from law enforcement sources thus must be supplemented with information from other sources (for example, investigations by independent journalists and scholars and by national and international bodies commissioned to look into this problem). We have drawn upon all of these sources in identifying what we see as some current problems in law, policy, procedure, and priorities.

Domestic Policy Issues

Great strides have been taken in the last 25 years against traditional (Cosa Nostra) forms of organized crime in the United States. This particular form of organized crime has been seriously weakened. Nevertheless, it has not been eliminated, and, more ominously, what is left of the old so-called "mafia" has been joined by a variety of increasingly powerful domestic and international organized criminal networks operating in the United States. A number of problems remain to be addressed in combating these groups.

■ Citizens have not been mobilized as allies in the effort to control organized crime. Despite a series of significant prosecutions for racketeering conspiracies during the past decade, vast numbers of Americans continue to gamble illegally, use banned drugs, buy stolen property, and otherwise contribute to the very same conspiracies that the Government is fighting to defeat.

■ Available scientific methods have not been employed to the greatest extent possible in developing investigative screening devices for organized crime cases. Case study findings on the infiltration of business by organized crime have not been translated into usable tools for investigators. Likewise, prediction models of businesses at high risk of such infiltration have not been tested.

■ An overlooked issue in the use of eavesdropping and monitoring devices (considered to be essential in investigating organized crime) is that Government agents are placed at considerable risk in placing such devices. Given that installation requires trespassing upon private property, beyond the risk of embarrassment at being caught, there is a real danger that a Government agent may be seen as an intruder and subjected to deadly defensive measures.

■ Criminal informants, who have become primary ingredients in organized crime prosecutions in recent years, must be more strictly controlled to prevent their misuse. There have been instances, especially at the local level, of the police being misled by informants, resulting in innocent people being harmed or killed. This undermines public support for the use of informants. The latter is especially important because informants are viewed skeptically by the public anyway. When the use of informants is abused, it only reinforces this skepticism in the minds of citizens who may be potential jurors in criminal cases involving informants.

■ There is an astounding lack of uniformity in the standards and quality of law enforcement training across the United States. This has a dramatic effect on the ability to investigate organized crime because incompetence and lack of professionalism are major factors in the failure to share intelligence information among the responsible agencies. Law enforcement agencies, often with good reason, simply refuse to share information with others because of suspicions about incompetence and corruption.

■ Legal provisions for asset forfeiture have been abused or misused by some law enforcement agencies. This creates a conflict of interest and offers temptations for self-serving actions.

■ There has been an increase in the number of clandestine drug laboratories in the United States. These laboratories produce synthetic drugs, such as methamphetamine and PCP, and combine coca leaves with solvents to produce cocaine. According to one estimate, illegal domestic laboratories are now capable of producing enough illicit drugs to satisfy U.S. consumers' demand. The Chemical Diversion and Trafficking Act established Federal recordkeeping, reporting, and transaction requirements for essential chemicals. However, only 18 States have enacted similar legislation to track chemicals, and this legislation varies widely in the number and types of chemicals covered and in drug-tracking requirements.

■ Court-imposed trusteeships on the Teamsters' and Laborers' unions have proven to be a uniquely effective way to remove "mob" influence from organizations where criminal prosecutions of leaders had no effect on the corrupt nature of these organizations in the past. This is because trustees have authority to control finances and other aspects of union operations, and they can ensure democratic elections of union officers. There are other non-union businesses presently controlled by organized crime that could benefit from such trusteeships.

■ There is too little interaction between law enforcement officials charged with investigating and prosecuting organized crime and criminologists who research the problem as a social phenomenon. Because of differences in organizational affiliations, they rarely or never meet at professional conferences. They also do not participate in any other forms of joint training, workshops, information-sharing forums, etc. In addition to maintaining a degree of ignorance on both sides, this isolation serves only to increase suspicion of the other group's motives. Opportunities to understand and better explain organized crime are lost as a result.

International Policy Issues

There is increasing evidence that the wealth and power of criminal organizations in various countries are growing and that there are international links among these organizations. A number of factors associated with this globalization of organized crime have implications for the United States:

■ A state of ungovernability, instability, and fragmentation in certain countries provides favorable conditions for the development and nurturance of organized criminal groups. This is especially true in the countries that were part of the former Soviet Union. But it is also arising in Eastern Europe and, for example, in Peru, Burma, Mexico, and Pakistan. These countries provide both bases of operation and safe havens for international criminals.

■ Criminal organizations are exploiting increases in immigration to the United States for both cover and concealment of criminal activities, as well as for recruitment. Groups from Latin America and China are heavily involved in alien smuggling. The Chinese are highly organized, and it is estimated that there are more than two dozen smuggling rings in New York City alone. Aliens are most often smuggled by boat and pay fees of up to $30,000 for their passage. This exorbitant passage fee makes them slaves to their transporters once they reach the United States. Because they are illegal aliens, they cannot work at regular jobs. As a result, they are exploited by unscrupulous employers or become active in prostitution, the drug trade, or other aspects of the illegal economy. In this way, victims become criminals themselves, thus adding to the crime problem. Interdiction at the U.S. borders does not seem to be effective.

■ Increased technology for communications, and increasingly sophisticated use of this technology, facilitates the use of wire transfers of money involved in money laundering on a much greater scale than ever before. The threat to the integrity of international banking is considerable.

■ Coupled with the vast increase in the scope and magnitude of the international organized crime problem is a woefully inadequate law enforcement response. This inadequacy arises from (1) lack of international cooperation and policy; (2) limited exchange of intelligence and mutual legal assistance; (3) functional and bureaucratic fragmentation among the various agencies of criminal justice; (4) absence of specialized personnel; (5) competition and turf battles among responsible agencies; and (6) a failure to coordinate or harmonize national and international laws.

Current developments in Eurasia exemplify the difficulties outlined above. There, law enforcement agencies are tainted by association with old regimes and old-style methods. There is confusion and duplication of effort involving old criminal codes, new legislation, and various administrative methods, both old and new. Personnel are not only suspect because of questionable integrity, they are also poorly trained and in short supply. In addition, there are widespread shortages of equipment, and available equipment is obsolete.

That these problems have not gone unrecognized by Federal law enforcement is evident in the efforts to establish an international training facility in Budapest, Hungary, to open a Federal Bureau of Investigation/Drug Enforcement Administration office in Beijing, and to increase resources for the Immigration and Naturalization Service. We applaud these initiatives as good beginnings.

Of continuing special concern, we believe, is the problem of organized crime operating in and from the former Soviet Union. What are termed, generically, "Russian mafia" are operating in Germany, Poland, and virtually every other state in Eastern and Central Europe. There is also a growing problem of organized criminal networks among Soviet emigres in the United States. In the successor states of the Soviet Union (especially Russia), organized crime is undermining efforts to create the rule of law as well as attacking various fledgling democratic institutions. It is likewise undermining popular attitudes toward democracy and free enterprise. Internationally, Russian organized crime's illegal trade in high-tech weaponry, potentially including nuclear weapons, constitutes a considerable threat.

Policy Recommendations

■ It is recommended that the special grand jury provisions of the Organized Crime Control Act finally be implemented. As you know, these provisions call for an investigative grand jury to be called at least every 18 months to examine organized crime and corruption in districts of more than 1 million citizens. Significantly, the law also provides for the special grand jury to issue a report on those conditions at the end of its term. This has rarely, if ever, occurred in the last 25 years. This omission misses a tremendous opportunity for citizens on the grand jury to help educate other citizens about the less obvious evils of organized crime. Rather than Government officials repeating what has been said since the days of Attorney General Robert Kennedy, fellow citizens would be mobilized to carry that same message through periodic grand jury reports, followup by town meetings, and other mechanisms to raise community awareness.

■ It is recommended that the Department of Justice sponsor one or more "teams" of interested researchers and organized crime investigators to work together for a period of months to test such investigative screening models and translate their findings into a usable form for investigators of organized crime at the Federal, State, and local levels. Such a case-screening, or business-screening, model could do much to reduce time spent on proactive investigations that lead to dead ends.

■ It is recommended that specific policy and judicial authorization guidelines be developed as a way to make installations of eavesdropping and monitoring devices uniform and the expectations of investigators, their supervisors, and the judiciary identical. There is no way to eliminate the danger of these installations, but law and policy must more specifically circumscribe this issue to protect those in law enforcement and to negate the possibility of agency embarrassment should an incident occur.

■ It is recommended that the Department of Justice establish a technical assistance program designed to train State and local agencies on the proper development, use, and management of criminal informants. This technical assistance might consist of development of police courses required for those handling informants, or inservice training, on this issue.

■ It is recommended that the Department of Justice develop minimum standards and curriculum for police training nationwide, with special emphasis on the training of local police. Inconsistency in training hurts professionalism, lateral career mobility of officers, and interagency cooperation in combating organized crime.

■ It is recommended that specific guidelines for seizures of assets be developed to set a national standard. Without such a standard, public confidence erodes when seizures are made that appear questionable. Several lawsuits against police are pending on this issue. A standard is imperative to remove the incidence or appearance of unprofessional behavior on the part of police in organized crime control efforts.

■ It is recommended that the Department of Justice provide incentives and guidelines for States, as well as other nations, to track identified illicit drugs and to prohibit their use under penalty of law. Other jurisdictions must also be kept abreast of new synthetic chemicals that should be added each year to the list of essential chemicals.

■ It is recommended that similar efforts be undertaken for nonunion businesses found to be controlled by organized crime. Such intervention enables the Government to "restart" the business with completely new personnel and supervisory and auditing procedures to prevent the return of organized crime. This kind of intercession in nonunion businesses has occurred in a few instances thus far, but its potential as a tool for long-term prevention is enormous.

■ It is recommended that the Department of Justice periodically sponsor long-term "prevention forums" for the specific purpose of integrating law enforcement and criminological perspectives on the problem of organized crime. There are expertise and insight on both sides that might prove valuable in the development of future innovations in organized crime control efforts.

■ The United States should take the lead in helping Russian officials to draft effective antiracketeering legislation. We do not believe that this legislation should necessarily be a duplicate of the Racketeer Influenced and Corrupt Organization (RICO) Act, but rather should be legislation that is appropriate to and mindful of Russia's special circumstances and legal traditions.

■ American and other Western aid to Russia should be targeted specifically toward combating organized crime. Steps to be taken in this effort must include reforming the Russian judicial system; equipping law enforcement with vehicles, computers, and other communications equipment; and providing training and technical assistance to law enforcement in organized crime investigative techniques. Consideration should also be given to some kind of salary supplementation plan. This aid must be linked to the development of aggressive methods for rooting out (and keeping out) corruption in the criminal justice system.

■ Establish a joint Western-Russian data bank on Russian organized crime. This data bank should include the names of individuals and groups known to be involved in organized crime, their criminal histories, records of international travel, their contacts in the West, their criminal enterprises and legitimate businesses, and other information. Interpol might do this, or at least play some role in it.

■ The intelligence gathering and investigative utility of the Financial Crimes Enforcement Network (FINCEN), already demonstrated in areas of international money laundering and banking schemes—especially those involving Russians—should be expanded.

■ A broad-based effort to improve the performance of criminal justice officials in the former Soviet Union—through recruitment, training, education, and technical assistance—should be undertaken. This effort should not be limited to include only agencies of the Federal Government such as the Federal Bureau of Investigation and the Drug Enforcement Administration; it should also draw heavily upon the resources and valuable expertise at the State and local levels. In addition, it should involve private sector organizations such as the Police Executive Research Forum, the Police Foundation, and the National District Attorneys Association, as well as criminology/criminal justice educators and researchers in colleges and universities.

Designing Out Crime

DESIGNING OUT CRIME

Issues

Summary

Our failure to bring crime under control through a wide range of modifications to the criminal justice system has blinded us to the successful efforts continuously being made by a host of private and public agencies—municipalities, schools, hospitals, parks, malls, bus companies, banks, department stores, taverns, offices, factories, parking lots—to bring a wide range of troublesome and costly crimes under control. In most cases, these successes are achieved by identifying ways to reduce opportunities for highly specific kinds of crime—the approach advocated by environmental crime prevention.

The essential tenets of environmental crime prevention, of which Crime Prevention Through Environmental Design (CPTED) and Situational Crime Prevention are the best known examples, are to:

- Increase the difficulty of committing crime (e.g., credit card photos).

- Increase the perceived risks (e.g., burglar alarms).

- Reduce the rewards associated with criminal acts (e.g., PIN for car radios).

- Reduce the rationalizations that facilitate crime (e.g., simplify tax forms).

While the Federal Government gave some support to CPTED in the 1970's, interest in environmental crime prevention languished in our country. One reason for this loss of support was the concern that blocking opportunities for crime would result in its displacement to some other target, time, or place (i.e., the net amount of crime would remain the same, although its manifestations would be different). This belief was bolstered by criminological theories that generally failed to recognize important situational determinants of crime, such as the availability of tempting goods to steal and the absence of adequate guardianship of vulnerable property and persons.

In recent years, however, new criminological theories have emphasized the role of opportunities in crime causation. These theories, which include routine activity theory and rational choice theory, argue that, as the number of opportunities for crime increase, more crimes will be committed; conversely, as opportunities are reduced, so crime will decline. Whether or not displacement takes place depends on the ease with which offenders can obtain the same criminal rewards without greatly increased effort or risks. Somebody who has developed the habit of shoplifting from the supermarket will not inevitably turn to some other form of crime, involving greater risk of detection and more severe penalties, if the store takes effective preventive action. In fact, particular crimes serve special purposes for the offender. A thwarted rapist will not turn to mugging or drug dealing.

Policy recommendations

- **Federal Crime Prevention Department.** A crime prevention department should be established in the Department of Justice along the lines of similar units now functioning in a number of European countries. This unit would have a research and dissemination role and would also initiate action to "design out crime" that more naturally falls to central government than to State or local agencies. For example, the department could ensure the security of the phone system, credit cards, or ATM cards through Federal influence on manufacturers and service providers at an industry level. Important preventive initiatives that currently need Federal Government sponsorship include development of effective personal alarms for repeat victims of domestic violence and the use of PIN numbers for VCR's and other electronic devices that are targets for burglary.

■ **Crime Prevention Extension Service.** A Crime Prevention Extension Service, linked to local universities, along the lines of the successful agricultural model, should be developed within the Department of Justice. Its mandate should be to deliver expert crime prevention advice to small businesses and local communities. Such a service would complement rather than compete with the work of the police, especially as community policing ideas take hold.

DESIGNING OUT CRIME

Introduction

Ever since crime rates began to rise in the 1960's, policymakers and criminologists have been searching for ways to bring crime under control. Unfortunately, we have focused too exclusively on the capacity of the criminal justice system to deter, incapacitate, or rehabilitate offenders. In the face of disappointing results, we have failed to look outside the criminal justice system, but rather have redoubled our efforts to achieve benefits the system probably cannot deliver. More police have been placed on the streets, more people have been arrested, more sentences have been lengthened, and more prisons have been built, all with little demonstrable benefit.

At the same time, unaided by policymakers and criminologists, a host of agencies and institutions outside the criminal justice system have been successfully making efforts to control a range of troublesome and costly crimes. These include efforts made by banks to prevent fraud and robbery, by department stores to reduce shoplifting, by transit systems to reduce graffiti, by municipalities to eliminate drug markets, by housing authorities to eliminate muggings, by schools to prevent bullying, by libraries to reduce book thefts, and by companies to reduce sexual harassment. Without these efforts, the crime problem would be truly out of hand.

Few of these successes have been studied, but the published literature contains case studies that document the following:

- The elimination of graffiti on the New York City subway system during the 1980's through a program of immediate cleansing of fresh attacks.

- The substantial reduction of aircraft hijackings in the 1970's achieved by baggage screening and associated measures at airports around the world.

- The virtual elimination of robberies of bus drivers in 20 U.S. cities during the 1970's following the introduction of exact fare.

- Substantially reduced levels of car theft in Germany, Great Britain, and the United States resulting from the introduction of steering locks in the 1960's and 1970's.

- Even greater reductions in car thefts in the early part of this century following the enactment of vehicle registration laws.

- Reductions in thefts of car radios following the introduction of security-coded radios that are operable only with knowledge of the PIN.

- Reductions in thefts from parking lots, robberies in subway stations, and graffiti and vandalism on buses, through the deployment of closed circuit television surveillance.

- Reduced assaults on bus drivers through the fitting of plexiglass screens.

- Greatly reduced shoplifting from stores and reduced book thefts from libraries after the adoption of electronic merchandise tagging.

- Reduced theft in hospitals of patients' belongings achieved by strict accounting systems and in warehouses by use of similar methods.

Reductions in crime occur relatively quickly after situational interventions, and the crimes prevented quickly turn into large savings, not just for those who would otherwise have been victims, but also for the public at large. For example, it has recently been estimated that for each burglary prevented in Canada that would have been solved, adjudicated, and followed by a prison sentence, the average saving to society per case would currently run around $160,000. There is little reason to think this figure would be very different in the United States.

The fast payoff from situational prevention efforts can be contrasted with that from other crime prevention strategies that often take years to produce reductions in crime if, indeed, they do at all. A classic example would be subsidized preschool programs (e.g., Operation Head Start) that intervene in the lives of 3- and 4-year-old children. If such programs work, presumably by changing a variety of attitudes or life and educational skills so that these children do not develop into persistent offenders during their teen and young adult years, the payoffs for expenditures now will occur during a period of 10 to 20 years in the future.

Principles of Designing Out Crime

Examples of successful efforts to reduce crime listed above show the great variety of crimes addressed and the methods employed, but in all cases the principles of situational prevention are the same. Preventive measures are focused on reducing opportunities for highly specific forms of crime. The identification and design of appropriate measures depend on a clear understanding of the ways in which offenders are permitted to accomplish their acts. What works in one situation and for one kind of crime will not necessarily work in other situations or for other kinds of crime. Even so, the wide variety of opportunity-reducing methods employed fall into 1 of 16 different categories serving 4 broad objectives of (1) increasing the difficulty of committing crime, (2) increasing the risks, (3) reducing the rewards, and (4) reducing the rationalizations that facilitate crime. These 16 techniques are listed in the table accompanying this submission, with examples of the application of each.

The essential tenets of environmental crime prevention are described above. Crime Prevention Through Environmental Design (CPTED) and Situational Crime Prevention are the best-known varieties. Although the Federal Government gave some support to CPTED in the 1970's, interest in environmental crime prevention has languished in this country, and the most recent developments have taken place in Canada, Australia, and parts of Europe, including Great Britain, where Situational Crime Prevention was developed. Environmental crime prevention now has a recognized policy role in these countries.

One reason for the decline of Federal support for CPTED was the concern that blocking opportunities for crime would result not in its elimination, but merely its displacement to some other target, time, or place. The net amount of crime would remain the same although its manifestations might be different.

This belief was bolstered by criminological theories that generally failed to recognize important situational determinants of crime, such as the availability of tempting goods to steal and the absence of adequate guardianship of vulnerable property and persons. An offender's attitudes and personality were thought to be the only really important determinants of crime.

In recent years, however, there has been rapid development of new criminological theories that emphasize the role of opportunities in crime causation. These theories, which include routine activity theory and rational choice theory, assert that, as the number of opportunities for crime increases, so will the number of crimes committed. Conversely, as the number of opportunities is reduced, crime will decline. Displacement is neither inevitable nor the most likely outcome. Whether or not it takes place depends on the ease with which offenders can obtain the same criminal rewards without greatly increasing their efforts or risks. Someone who has developed the habit of shoplifting from the local supermarket will not inevitably turn to another form of crime, involving greater risk of detection and more severe penalties, if the store takes effective preventive action. Although opportunities for crime may seem boundless, in fact, particular crimes serve special purposes for the offender. For example, a thwarted rapist will not turn to mugging or drug dealing.

Displacement has been very extensively studied during the past decade, and a review of 55 separate research studies undertaken for the Dutch Ministry of Justice (1994) reached conclusions consistent with these theoretical arguments. The review found no evidence of displacement in 22 of the studies. In the remaining 33, some displacement of crime was reported, but in no case was it complete. This conclusion has been echoed in literature reviews undertaken in Great Britain, Canada, and the United States.

The Federal Government Role

This characterization of environmental crime prevention raises the important question of what role, if any, the Federal Government has in a form of crime control that relies so much on local action by municipalities, transit authorities, schools, housing authorities, hospitals, airports, stores, corporations, and

Table 1: Sixteen Techniques of Situational Crime Control With Examples

Increasing Perceived Effort	Increasing Perceived Risks	Reducing Anticipated Rewards	Inhibiting Rationalizations
1. *Target hardening:* Steering locks Bandit screens	5. *Entry/exit screening:* Baggage screening Merchandise tags	9. *Target removal:* Removable car radio Exact change fares	13. *Facilitating compliance:* Trash bins Simplified tax forms
2. *Access control:* Fenced yards Entry phones	6. *Formal surveillance:* Burglar alarms Security guards	10. *Identifying property:* Property marking Vehicle licensing	14. *Controlling disinhibitors:* Ignition interlock Server intervention
3. *Deflecting offenders:* Tavern location School location	7. *Surveillance by employees:* Park attendants Receptionists	11. *Reducing temptation:* Gender-neutral phone lists Concealing valuables	15. *Rule setting:* Customs declaration Hotel registrations
4. *Controlling facilitators:* Credit card photo Ignition interlock	8. *Natural surveillance:* Defensible space Neighborhood watch	12. *Denying benefits:* Graffiti cleaning PIN for car radios	16. *Increasing informal sanctions:* Shoplifting a crime Roadside speedometers

businesses. Does the Government need to be involved in efforts that are already successful?

These questions can best be answered by examining the experience of such countries as the Netherlands, Great Britain, and Sweden, where central governments have established dedicated units within their departments of justice to promote environmental crime prevention. These units serve a variety of roles. They encourage research and dissemination of good practices so that ideas that have worked in one town or one agency are tried elsewhere. These units also identify opportunities for the central government to take action. For example, all experts agree that the most effective way to reduce car theft is to persuade vehicle manufacturers to produce more secure vehicles. This is not a matter for a local municipality or police department. Effective action would also be difficult to take at a State level. Rather, this task falls to the Federal Government, and many similar opportunities exist to influence manufacturers and service providers at an industry level. The security of the telephone system, credit cards, and automatic teller machines are primary examples. To take proper advantage of these opportunities, we would propose that a crime prevention department based on the European model be established in the U.S. Department of Justice.

There are currently important preventive opportunities in the development of effective personal alarms for repeat victims of domestic violence and the use of PIN numbers for VCR's and other electronic equipment that are the targets for burglary. Both of these initiatives need Government sponsorship and might be candidates for priority action by the Federal crime prevention department we have proposed.

A Crime Prevention Extension Service

The government crime prevention units recently established in various European countries are successfully disseminating good practices. These countries have highly centralized governments, however, and they are much smaller than the United States. Different structures for disseminating good practices may be necessary here, and we would propose the establishment of a crime prevention extension service along the lines of the agricultural model that has served this country so well. Various local private and public agencies with crime problems will be able to seek or be offered

assistance from this service without having to comply with any orders or demands. The service would offer nothing more than suggestions. At first only a few agencies will adopt innovations; if they work, others will join. Thus, the proposed service would be well attuned to the population and compatible with the existing U.S. Government structure.

Since crime is disproportionately a metropolitan problem, a crime prevention extension service should begin in metropolitan areas in conjunction with metropolitan universities. Perhaps most importantly, a crime prevention extension service should be linked to a criminology or criminal justice department, yet it should be administered with a clear mandate to assist people in the community to prevent crime. Within the university, the service may also foster ties to such academic departments as business, architecture, hotel management, parks administration, hospital administration, and other departments that train people in practical industries with crime problems, so long as practical crime prevention remains the central focus. In time, the agricultural extension service might join in carrying crime prevention ideas to rural areas.

It is essential that the crime prevention extension service not be distracted by the usual "soft" types of crime prevention, such as public relations for police departments, "officer friendly" programs to meet with school children, and lectures on the need for more education or social programs. These methods are soft because they are designed to meet, with very little thought, the political demands of anxious people rather than to encourage true crime prevention based on knowledge or experience. Instead, a crime prevention extension service must focus on solving specific problems in specific settings, perhaps expanding to include the design of nearby environments.

The central focus of these efforts should be private businesses, especially small businesses, that are the heart and core of crime prevention. Examples of businesses to be served by a crime prevention extension service include small shop owners confronting shoplifting, bar owners dealing with fights and drunkenness, small factory owners concerned with danger in the parking lots, and other companies trying to prevent graffiti, vandalism, and break-ins. However, such a service should not be limited to businesses; it should also include churches, neighborhood associations, condominium associations, block clubs, downtown associations, and those organizations whose efforts can prevent crime against themselves, their customers, or others in the vicinity. In addition, services can be provided to municipal governments, zoning boards, and others in the planning process; park administrations; schools; or additional public and quasi-public agencies.

The Fit With Community Policing

Many police departments may initially have little interest in the proposed extension services or would claim that they have always provided these services anyway. It is true that crime prevention offices are found within police departments, but these offices are often linked to public relations. Thus, they have more of a political function than a serious crime prevention function. Moreover, their repertoire of crime prevention ideas is generally narrow: lock your doors, buy an alarm, and don't go out too late.

However, change is occurring in more and more police departments. In particular, the concept of problem-oriented policing is spreading. This means seeking to direct police activity toward an understanding and analysis of "the problem" and toward finding ways to change the conditions giving rise to crime, rather than arresting offenders without an overall strategy. This concept is compatible with environmental crime prevention, and many ideas from this field should filter naturally into the problem-oriented approach to policing. As the repertoire of prevention ideas develops and as police departments themselves broaden their repertoire, we envision much greater cooperation and interchange between the crime prevention extension services and police agencies. In time, therefore, the extension service could fill a valuable role in the development of community policing in this country.

The State of the Police

THE STATE OF THE POLICE

Summary

Issues

The most visible trend in policing today is the move to community- and problem-oriented models of policing (COP/POP). One thing is already clear: as local police forces adopt COP/POP, care must be taken to ensure that both police responsiveness and police accountability are enhanced. Responsiveness demands sensitivity to the concerns of local communities, while accountability demands police adherence to an overriding ethic of constitutionality and law. Unfortunately, public anxiety about crime and disorder can shift the balance. In times of great social change, responsiveness often overrides accountability, as long-term constitutional guarantees and due process safeguards are abandoned or watered down in ill-advised attempts to provide quick fixes. It is important to avoid any methods that could permanently reduce police accountability when responding to public concerns about crime, violence, and drugs.

Traditional professions such as law and medicine have struck a balance between responsiveness and accountability that the police should emulate. What the police lack is a meaningful standard of care for police operations. For example, police manuals rarely tell officers how to respond to a crime in progress. In many departments, an officer's discretion in arrests, except for those involving domestic abuse, is not subject to official guidelines. Few agencies have meaningful guidelines on how to handle mentally or emotionally disturbed people. And police vehicle pursuit standards vary from one jurisdiction to another.

Given the gravity, urgency, and potentially catastrophic results of many police field decisions, the absence of a standard is an omission of major import. It is comparable to a situation in which medical researchers, scholars, and practitioners had concentrated on hospital administration issues and neglected to develop and disseminate information about treatment techniques and strategies.

The consequences of being without an operational standard include incomplete recruiting and training of police officers, inadequate or nonexistent postemployment training, and insufficient or unrealistic criteria on which to assess the quality of police performance. Resentment can grow between police, who feel they have been unfairly criticized, and the community, which feels its members have been poorly treated.

Policy recommendations

- **Endorse COP/POP initiatives.** To the extent that COP/POP involves a partnership between the police and the community, the initiatives should be vigorously supported and periodically refined.

- **Support hiring new officers.** Hiring 100,000 new officers under the 1994 Crime Law strongly supports COP/POP initiatives; there is no way to increase police visibility and interaction with the community without a significant number of additional officers. However, while the police can be active in attempting to build community, this task requires great work at all levels of government and society.

- **Develop standard of care.** A standard of care for police operations, which includes devising means of providing citizen input into both formulation and implementation of policy, should be systematically developed and disseminated. The first step is developing a methodology to help police, the public, and government officials identify desirable, realistic outcomes of police work, the means most likely to attain these outcomes, and techniques for evaluating performance in terms of these goals.

- **Increase civilian advisory boards.** The trend toward civilian police advisory boards and review panels appears to be completely in line with the philosophies and logic underlying COP/POP. The boards need to be rigorously evaluated to determine what effect they have on policing and police-community relations and which of the boards' methods succeed or fail.

- **Oppose exceptions to the exclusionary rule.** Good-faith exceptions or other modifications that would weaken the exclusionary rule in evaluating a police officer's actions should be eliminated. "Good faith" clauses tend to encourage and even reward police incompetence and failure to learn fundamental constitutional principles. They wrongly assume that courts can identify officers who act in bad faith. Experience teaches that people who act in bad faith rarely testify in good faith about their misconduct. In every field of human endeavor, the major purpose of education, training, and discipline is to replace good faith mistakes with adherence to professional standards.

- **Combat police abuse.** The custom-and-practice authority granted to the Justice Department in the 1994 Crime Law is an invaluable means of combating police abuse. The provision eliminates the requirement that the Civil Rights Division of the Justice Department have "standing" as an injured party to initiate civil litigation against police for brutality or other unconstitutional misconduct.

- **Perform analyses of causes of crime.** Meaningful analysis of the social and economic causes of crime and disorder should be conducted to develop a comprehensive approach to dealing with them. In many instances, new officers, who were hired to enhance community relations, may find no community exists. The police cannot rebuild communities by themselves.

- **Expand evaluation research.** The Federal Government should continue and expand support for evaluation research of policing and dissemination of its findings, with emphasis on: implementation of community- and problem-oriented policing, crime causation and prevention, development of a standard of care, accountability issues discussed here, gun detection, and police leadership.

THE STATE OF THE POLICE

Overview

This task force was convened in October 1994 at the request of American Society of Criminology President Freda Adler. The mandate of the task force was to describe and critique the current state of policing in the United States and make suggestions for future directions in police policy, operations, and research.

The task force's principal conclusions and recommendations focus primarily on action that may be taken at the Federal level.

They are:

- To the extent that the concept of community- and problem-oriented models of policing (COP/POP) involves a partnership between the police and the community, rather than a continuation of the estrangement that has often characterized relations between police and community, we support it vigorously and recommend continued efforts to refine it.

- We recommend development and dissemination of a standard of care for police operations.

- We vigorously oppose any good-faith exceptions or other modifications that would weaken the exclusionary rule.

- We strongly endorse the custom-and-practice authority granted to the U.S. Department of Justice in the 1994 Crime Law.

- We support the trend to civilian police advisory boards and review panels.

- We strongly support the 1994 Crime Law's plan to hire 100,000 officers committed to COP/POP, but:

  - We vigorously oppose any suggestion that the addition of these officers for COP/POP is the only solution to the problems of crime and disorder now plaguing the United States.

  - We recommend meaningful analysis of the social and economic causes of crime and disorder and the development of a comprehensive approach to dealing with them.

- We recommend that the Federal Government continue to expand support for evaluation research and dissemination of its findings—with emphasis on implementation of community- and problem-oriented policing, crime causation and prevention, development of a standard of care, the accountability issues discussed in this paper, gun detection, and police leadership.

Policing in 1995

Clearly, the most visible trend in policing today is the move to community- and problem-oriented models of policing (COP/POP). To the extent that COP/POP involves a partnership between the police and the community, rather than a continuation of the estrangement that has often characterized relations between police and community, we support it vigorously and recommend continued efforts to refine it.

Responsiveness and accountability. As policing moves toward adoption of COP/POP, care must be taken to assure that both police responsiveness and police accountability are enhanced. Responsiveness demands sensitivity to the concerns of local communities, while accountability demands police adherence to an overriding ethic of constitutionality and law. The priority order of these two considerations should be clear and unvarying: accountability should never be sacrificed in the name of responsiveness. Unfortunately, especially in times of great social change, responsiveness often overrides accountability, as long-term constitutional guarantees and due process safeguards are abandoned or watered down in ill-advised attempts to provide quick fixes to increased public anxiety about crime and disorder. This is such a time and, later in this report, we make several specific recommendations involving the need to avoid responding to current public concerns about crime, violence, and drugs in ways that permanently reduce police accountability.

The Need To Develop an Operational Standard of Care

The traditional professions—law and medicine—have struck a balance between responsiveness and accountability that should be emulated by the police. The first step in this direction involves the development and dissemination of a meaningful standard of care for police operations. This includes devising means of encouraging citizen input into both the formulation of policy[1] and the manner in which it is implemented. The absence of such a standard is a major cause of police-community friction and violence, and it contributes greatly to the stress, frustrations, and anger among rank-and-file officers.

There is, by now, a long bookshelf of research, theorizing, and law that has profoundly and positively affected the manner in which police administrators deploy officers and use their other resources. Unfortunately, except for legislative and judicial interventions, surprisingly little effort has been devoted to guiding officers' discretion in the field. Existing police professional standards, such as those of the Commission on Accreditation for Law Enforcement Agencies, Inc., deal primarily with administrative issues rather than with the direct delivery of police services by line officers. Given the gravity, urgency, and potentially catastrophic results of many police field decisions, this is an omission of major dimensions: it is as though medical researchers, scholars, and practitioners had concentrated on hospital administration issues and neglected to develop and disseminate information about treatment techniques and strategies.

The lack of focus on street-level policing is also ironic considering that what little has been done has been so successful. Despite the increased violence on U.S. streets over the past few decades, administrative rules governing officers' use of deadly force (and enhanced tactical training) have greatly reduced bloodshed between police and citizens, as has the development of tactics and strategies for hostage and barricade situations.

For many critical operations in many police agencies, attempts to develop standards of care have been isolated or never undertaken. For example:

■ Police manuals rarely tell officers how to respond to crimes in progress.

■ Officers' arrest discretion, especially—but not solely—in situations excluding domestic abuse, is not often subject to any official guidance.

■ Many agencies provide officers with no meaningful guidance about how to handle encounters with mentally or emotionally disturbed persons and violent subjects without using more force than necessary.

■ Police vehicle pursuit standards have been developed, but they vary dramatically and even are contradictory in some places. The attorney general of New Jersey, for example, issued a directive that, for all intents and purposes, prohibits officers from engaging in pursuits of traffic violators. A few months later, the State's supreme court gave its imprimatur to such chases as long as they do not involve demonstrably reckless police behavior.[2]

Consequences of the missing standard of care. The absence of an operational standard of care has major effects:

■ The knowledge, skills, and abilities necessary to do the police job well cannot be described with any reasonable degree of precision. Consequently:

❑ Police recruiting and training generally are inexact, least-common-denominator processes that cannot be objectively validated.

❑ Existing hiring standards are not comparable to those of occupations with apparently similar line-level decisionmaking authority and responsibility (e.g., teachers, social workers, prosecutors, public defenders, and probation and parole officers). Instead, police are most often equated with fire and sanitation workers, who have dangerous jobs but little decisionmaking responsibility.

❑ Postemployment training of U.S. police officers is nonexistent in many places (especially rural areas) and, virtually everywhere, it is minimal.

U.S. police serve the most heterogenous and well-armed population in the world but receive less (and less consistent) training than police in other western democracies.

■ Much police work is done on an ad hoc basis, rather than on the basis of clearly enunciated standards.

■ The most critical police decisions become on-the-spot judgment calls. These frequently result in mistakes—real or perceived—that subject the police to criticism and liability for violating vague professional standards and lead the courts to fashion the industry standard of care.

■ Resentment grows between police, who feel that they have been unfairly criticized, and the community, which feels that its members have been poorly treated.

■ Administrators have no meaningful standards for evaluating officers.

■ Citizens and government officials have no meaningful standards for assessing the quality of police services, and:

❏ Often have unrealistic views of what police can accomplish.

❏ Often are frustrated with police service because of problems that cannot possibly be solved by the police (e.g., they blame police for levels of violence police cannot reasonably be expected to affect).

❏ Accept baseless police claims that reductions in crime are attributable to police overaggressiveness, coming to equate tough policing with effectiveness and regarding more realistic and humane styles of policing as ineffective and soft on crime.

Developing a standard of care. Given the great diversity among communities served by U.S. police departments, we recognize that it may not be possible to develop a universal statement of the role of the police. At the same time, we recommend development and dissemination of a standard of care for police operations. This should begin with construction of a

methodology that helps police and the consumers of their services (i.e., officials and the public) to identify:

■ Desirable and realistic outcomes of police work.

■ The means most likely to attain these outcomes.

■ Methods of evaluating police performance in terms of the extent to which desirable outcomes are attained and/or (especially in hopeless cases) the extent to which police have followed the methods most likely to result in success.

Accountability

As suggested above, our experience as social scientists and police practitioners leads to several extremely important recommendations related to accountability. There is a temptation to "take the handcuffs off the police" when there is great public concern about crime and violence. This should be avoided because there is no evidence that such handcuffs hinder the crimefighting ability of the police. No study has ever shown that any United States Supreme Court decision, for example, has ever affected police effectiveness or public safety in any way. Instead, these decisions serve only the critical functions of defining the extent of citizens' freedoms.

Consequently, we vigorously oppose any good-faith exceptions or other modifications that would weaken the exclusionary rule. As scholars, we have seen no research that shows that the exclusionary rule results in dismissals or acquittals in more than 2 percent of criminal prosecutions. In addition, proposals for good-faith exceptions are fatally flawed in their assumption that courts can identify officers who act in bad faith: people who act in bad faith rarely testify in good faith about their misconduct. We strongly endorse the custom-and-practice authority granted to the U.S. Department of Justice in the 1994 Crime Law. In effect, this provision of the new law eliminates the requirement that the Civil Rights Division of the U.S. Department of Justice has "standing" as an injured party to initiate civil litigation against police for brutality or other unconstitutional misconduct. This is an invaluable means of combating police abuse, and we welcome it.

CRITICAL CRIMINAL JUSTICE ISSUES

We support the trend to civilian police advisory boards and review panels. The recent widespread adoption of these review mechanisms is evidence of growing recognition that they are proper, needed, and completely in accord with the philosophies and logic underlying COP/POP. We urge evaluation of the effects of these boards on policing and police-community relations as well as research to determine what distinguishes between success and failure in the operation of these boards.

Community- and Problem-Oriented Policing

To the extent that COP/POP requires more—and less adversarial—interaction between police and community, we strongly support the 1994 Crime Law's plan to hire 100,000 officers committed to COP/POP. Over the last generation, police workload (calls for service, street crime, and disorder) has increased dramatically both in number and complexity. During the same period, personnel resources in much of the country have not increased, especially when one controls for the reduced working hours (usually from 48 hours a week to 40 hours a week) won by police labor groups. There is no way to increase police visibility and interaction with the community without a significant number of additional officers.

In making this recommendation we recognize that, like past proposals and anticipated panaceas, neither COP/POP nor the addition of 100,000 officers can solve all the problems we ask police to address. The success of community policing depends in large measure on the strength of the community involved as well as on the capabilities of the police. Unfortunately, the jurisdictions most in need of community policing are not strong communities in the traditional sense. In such places, whatever community exists is often estranged from the police. Certainly the police can be active in attempting to build community, but this is a task that requires great work at all levels of government and society. We note, for example, that "hate crime" is a troubling apparent trend in many pluralistic and/or "changing" communities. This certainly strikes a community at its core and weakens any COP/POP operations. We need to know more about it and what to do about it if COP/POP is to succeed.

Thus, we vigorously oppose any suggestion that the addition of 100,000 officers for COP/POP is a comprehensive approach to the problems of crime and disorder now plaguing the United States. Such a view ignores the fact that, unlike courts and corrections, police services (especially under COP/POP models) include much that is not directly related to crime. Worse, such a view is a distraction from the social and economic causes of crime and disorder that must be addressed in any meaningful approach to what are now viewed as police problems. The addition of more officers to the ranks of the police should not be an excuse to avoid doing this. These new officers may be necessary if COP/POP is to be implemented. More importantly, however, we recommend meaningful analysis of the social and economic causes of crime and disorder and development of a comprehensive approach to dealing with them.

Evaluation Research

Police throughout the United States are engaged in all sorts of innovative programs and operations. We have encountered a wide variety of imaginative COP/POP-based quality-of-life and fear-of-crime programs in urban jurisdictions, but their effects are unknown. Almost certainly, there also are many innovative programs among smaller, more flexible rural agencies that, without articulating it, have long been involved in COP/POP, but the isolation of these agencies keeps their successes a secret. Police in some jurisdictions suspect—but do not know—that recent decreases in crimes typically committed by juveniles may be associated with increased enforcement of truancy laws. One agency has provided joggers and other volunteers with cellular phones that can be used to summon police quickly to crimes or other emergencies that they might observe in parks and other public places; no analysis of the results is in progress.

Absent such analysis, it is impossible to isolate the effects of these programs. Absent publication, police agencies are precluded from learning from the experiences of their colleagues in other places. In the current fiscal environment, local jurisdictions frequently consider formal evaluation and publication of results to be an expensive luxury. Such a view is unfortunate but perhaps understandable at the local level where officials are primarily concerned with their own constituencies. It should not prevail at the Federal level, however, where official concern should extend to all Americans. In recent years, however, Federal funding for police research and publication has been virtually nil, typically averaging about 7 cents per American per year. Given the prominence of crime and justice issues on the national political scene as well as the disproportionately great and positive impact of what has been done, this is a major default.

Among federally funded police research currently in progress, we are particularly optimistic about the potential results of work designed to assist police in finding illegal concealed weapons. We urge that this work continue and that it be conducted in ways that adhere to constitutional standards. In addition to a much needed focus on the line level of policing, research and evaluation should also examine police leadership and the executive, managerial, and supervisory qualities and strategies most closely associated with successful policing (once success is adequately defined, of course). Thus, we recommend that the Federal Government continue to expand support for evaluation research and dissemination of its findings with emphasis on implementation of community- and problem-oriented policing, crime causation and prevention, development of a standard of care, the accountability issues discussed in this paper, gun detection, and police leadership. Research and evaluation findings should be broadly disseminated to practitioners by the U.S. Department of Justice through, for example, Research in Brief reports and regional meetings.

Notes

1. As we define it, a police operational standard of care is a systematically developed and disseminated body of knowledge, similar to those of the traditional professions and such emergency occupations as the fire service and aviation. It should provide meaningful guidance to line personnel who face the need to make critical decisions. As such, it cannot be a set of hard-and-fast rules, which would unreasonably limit line discretion. Instead, it is a set of goal-oriented guidelines to be developed, applied, and enforced under the criteria of objective reasonableness historically employed in these other vocations.

2. We are well aware that some of our criticisms appear contrary to practices described in much of the scholarly literature of policing and that our comments do not apply to each and every U.S. police agency. At the same time, we are confident that our observations apply to most American policing and caution that it is risky to generalize from the departments studied by scholars to the universe of U.S. police agencies. By definition, police agencies cited in the literature differ from all others: they have opened their books, records, operations, and personnel to outsiders. Consequently, as our occasional opportunities to study agencies that have been involuntary research subjects corroborate, agencies that have volunteered to cooperate with research may generally be presumed to be both more progressive and more confident of their practices than are agencies that have remained closed to scrutiny.

A Crime Control Rationale for Reinvesting in Community Corrections

A CRIME CONTROL RATIONALE FOR REINVESTING IN COMMUNITY CORRECTIONS

Summary

Issues

Two years ago Congress passed the most ambitious crime bill in the Nation's history, the Violent Crime Control and Law Enforcement Act of 1994. It allocated $22 billion to expand prisons, impose longer sentences, hire more police, and, to a lesser extent, fund prevention programs. The bill was later amended, and nearly all of the $5 billion targeted for prevention programs was diverted into prison construction and law enforcement. Although such tough-on-crime legislation has political appeal, it finds almost no support among criminal justice practitioners and scholars.

Recently, organizations as diverse as the International Association of Chiefs of Police, the U.S. Conference of Mayors, the American Bar Association, the National Governors Association, the League of Cities, the RAND Corporation, the National Council on Crime and Delinquency, the Campaign for an Effective Crime Policy, and the National Research Council have all voiced opposition to the approach. In addition, 85 percent of nationally surveyed prison wardens—who stand to benefit by this legislation—said that elected officials are not offering effective solutions to America's crime problem.

Some people argue that the current proposals are racist or that they cost too much; however, nearly everyone agrees that they fail to prevent young people from entering and continuing a life of crime, and they leave the vast majority of criminals, who are serving sentences on probation and parole, unaffected.

Criminologists have long observed that age 18 is the year of peak criminality. Analysis recently completed by Alfred Blumstein at Carnegie-Mellon University showed that today's cohort of 18- year-olds is the smallest it will be for at least the next 15 years. In 1996 the number is going to start climbing, and the biggest growth will occur in the number of African-American children who are now 4 to 9 years old. As more young people are recruited into and retained in a criminal lifestyle, the ability of back-end responses (such as imprisonment) to increase public safety is severely limited because of the replenishing supply of young people who are entering into criminal careers.

The second, and equally important, reason why current Federal efforts will fail is that they focus exclusively on prisons as a corrections strategy, ignoring the fact that most criminals are serving probation and parole sentences. In 1991 about 16 percent of all adult probationers were convicted of violent crimes, as were 26 percent of parolees. This means that on any given day in 1991, there were resident in U.S. communities an estimated 435,000 probationers and 155,000 parolees who had been convicted of violent crimes. In contrast to these 590,000 probationers and parolees in the community, only 372,500 violent offenders resided in prison. And in 1993, 72 percent of all identified criminals were serving sentences in the community, on probation or parole. Even though the number of prisons has quadrupled in the past decade, prisoners are still less than one-fifth of the convict population, and the vast majority of offenders remain in the community. If effectively controlling crime—as opposed to exacting retribution and justice—is the goal, efforts must be focused on the community, where offenders are reporting to probation and parole officers.

Probationers represent a serious continued risk to public safety. The majority of probationers are convicted felons, have prior criminal records, and are likely to be substance and alcohol abusers with few marketable skills. Continued indifference to their behavior means missing the opportunity to intervene positively—and promises their eventual imprisonment. In addition, by not focusing on providing probationers with an appropriate level and type of supervision, crime in the community will not be abated. Current policy simply waits until their criminality escalates to the point of incarceration, which has been proven to be costly and ineffective in reducing crime.

Policy recommendations

■ **"Surveillance plus treatment" programs.** Such programs should be developed for drug-involved probationers, including offenders who are convicted of drug possession and use. Program models now exist that are effective in reducing recidivism rates, and the public supports rehabilitation over incarceration for such offenders (but not drug traffickers). The cost-benefit tradeoff between prison and community corrections is among the highest for this subpopulation.

■ **Convincing the public.** The public's trust that probation and parole can be meaningful, credible sanctions must be regained. During the past decade, many jurisdictions developed "intermediate sanctions" as a response to prison crowding. These programs (e.g., house arrest, electronic monitoring, intensive supervision) were designed to be community-based sanctions that were tougher than regular probation, but less stringent and expensive than prison. In the few instances where the organizational capacity was created to ensure compliance with court-ordered conditions, these programs reduced recidivism by 20 to 30 percent.

■ **Funding.** Sufficient financial resources must be provided so that the designed programs, combining both treatment and surveillance, can be implemented. Adequate monetary resources are essential to obtaining and sustaining judicial support and achieving program success. The resources needed will be forthcoming only if the public believes the programs are both effective and punishing.

A CRIME CONTROL RATIONALE FOR REINVESTING IN COMMUNITY CORRECTIONS

Introduction and Overview

Two years ago Congress passed the most ambitious crime bill in our Nation's history, the Violent Crime Control and Law Enforcement Act of 1994. It allocated $22 billion to expand prisons, impose longer sentences, hire more police, and, to a lesser extent, fund prevention programs. But as part of the Republicans' "Contract with America," the Act was significantly revised, and the money allocated to prevention programs was scrapped. The amended bill—the price tag of which rose to $30 billion— shifted nearly all of the $5 billion targeted for prevention programs into prison construction and law enforcement. As a *Los Angeles Times* opinion piece concluded of the whole matter: "what started out last legislative season as a harsh and punitive bill has gotten downright Draconian" (Schiraldi, 1995).

While such tough-on-crime legislation has political appeal, it finds almost no support among criminal justice practitioners and scholars. They are uniformly agreed that such efforts—which endorse an "enforcement model" to the sacrifice of all else—will do little to curb crime. In recent months organizations as diverse as the International Association of Chiefs of Police (IACP), the U.S. Conference of Mayors, the American Bar Association (ABA), the National Governors Association, the League of Cities, the RAND Corporation, the National Council on Crime and Delinquency (NCCD), the Campaign for an Effective Crime Policy (CECP), and the National Research Council have all voiced opposition to the approach.

Even prison wardens (who stand to win) uniformly reject the crime-fighting solutions coming out of Washington. In a recent national survey of prison wardens, 85 percent of those surveyed said that elected officials are not offering effective solutions to America's crime problem (Simon, 1994). Chase Riveland, Washington State director of corrections, said that focusing only on prisons and ignoring the rest of the system is "drive-by legislation, at best." And Jerome Skolnick, president of the American Society of Criminology (ASC), spoke of the Federal efforts in his 1994 presidential address and entitled the speech, "What Not to Do About Crime."

What is wrong with the current proposals? Some argue that they are racist, others argue that they cost too much, but nearly everyone agrees they have two major flaws: (1) they fail to prevent young people from entering and continuing a life of crime, and (2) they leave the vast majority of criminals, who are serving sentences on probation and parole, unaffected.

Criminologists have long observed that age 18 is the year of peak criminality. Analysis recently completed by Alfred Blumstein at Carnegie-Mellon showed that today we have the smallest cohort of 18-year-olds we will see for at least the next 15 years. In 1996, the number is going to start going up, and the biggest growth will occur in the number of African-American children who are now 4 to 9 years old. Blumstein (1994) recently observed:

> These young people are being less well educated and socialized, and as a result are easy recruits for the booming crack cocaine industry, where weapons are a business accessory for an increasing number of youths. The result will be a steep increase in juvenile and young adult violent crime, unless we begin investing in community-based programs to better socialize kids when their parents are not doing so. This is a population crying out for our attention, and, as a society we need to find a means to divert them from becoming as violent as their big brothers.

As more young people are recruited into and retained in a criminal lifestyle, the ability of back-end responses (such as imprisonment) to increase public safety is severely limited because of the replenishing supply of young people who are entering into criminal careers.

regarding program effectiveness. Targeting drug offenders makes the most sense for a number of reasons. Drug offenders were not always punished so frequently by imprisonment. In California, for example, just 5 percent of convicted drug offenders were sentenced to prison in 1980, but by 1990 the number had increased to 20 percent. The large-scale imprisonment of drug offenders has only recently taken place, and there is some new evidence suggesting that the public seems ready to shift its punishment strategies for low-level drug offenders.

A 1994 nationwide poll by Hart Research Associates reported that Americans have come to understand that drug abuse is not simply a failure of willpower or a violation of criminal law. They now see the problem as far more complex, involving not only individual behavior but also fundamental issues of poverty, opportunity, and personal circumstances. Drug Strategies, a nonprofit policy organization based in Washington, D.C., reported in 1995 that nearly half of all Americans have been touched directly by the drug problem: 45 percent of those surveyed in the 1994 Hart poll said that they know someone who became addicted to a drug other than alcohol. This personal knowledge is changing attitudes about how to deal with the problem: 7 in 10 believed that their addicted acquaintance would have been helped more by entering a supervised treatment program than by being sentenced to prison.

It appears that the public now wants tougher sentences for drug traffickers and more treatment for addicts. What legislators have given them instead are long sentences for everyone. Drug Strategies, which analyzed the Hart survey, concluded that "public opinion on drugs is more pragmatic and less ideological than the current political debate reflects. Voters know that punitive approaches won't work." So, in that vein, the public appears willing to accept something other than prison for some drug offenders.

The public's receptiveness to treatment for addicts is important because those familiar with delivering treatment say that is where treatment can make the biggest impact. A recent report by the prestigious Institute of Medicine (IOM) recommends focusing on probationers and parolees to curb drug use and related crime. They noted that about one-fifth of the population estimated to need treatment—and two-fifths of those

clearly needing it—are under the supervision of the justice system as parolees or probationers. And because the largest single group of serious drug users in any locality comes through the justice system every day, the IOM concludes that the justice system is one of the most important gateways to treatment delivery and should be used more effectively.

Moreover, those under corrections supervision stay longer in treatment, thereby increasing positive treatment outcomes. The claim that individuals forced into treatment by the courts will not be successful has not been borne out by research. In fact, just the opposite is true. The largest study of drug treatment outcomes (TOPS) found that justice system clients stayed in treatment longer than clients with no justice system involvement. As a result, they had higher than average success rates.

However, as noted above, quality treatment does not come cheap. But in terms of crime and health costs averted, it is an investment that pays for itself immediately. Researchers in California recently conducted an assessment of drug treatment programs and identified those that were successful, concluding that it can now be "documented that treatment and recovery programs are a good investment" (Gerstein et al., 1994). The researchers studied a sample of 1,900 treatment participants, followed them up for as long as 2 years of treatment, and studied participants from the four major treatment modalities: therapeutic communities, social model, outpatient drug-free, and methadone maintenance. Gerstein et al. (1994: 33) concluded:

> Treatment was very cost-beneficial: for every dollar spent on drug and alcohol treatment, the State of California saved $7 in reductions in crime and health care costs. The study found that each day of treatment *paid for itself on the day treatment was received*, primarily through an avoidance of crime.

The level of criminal activity declined by two-thirds from before treatment to after treatment. The greater the length of time spent in treatment, the greater the reduction in crime. Reported criminal activity declined before and after treatment as follows: mean number of times sold or helped sell drugs (-75 percent), mean number of times used weapon/physical force (-93 percent), percent

The second, and equally important, reason why current Federal efforts will fail is that they focus exclusively on prisons as a corrections strategy, ignoring the fact that most criminals are serving probation and parole sentences. In 1993 there were just under 5 million adult (convicted) criminals—or about 1 in every 39 Americans. Seventy-two percent of all identified criminals were not in prison, but serving sentences in the community on probation or parole supervision. Even though we have quadrupled the number of prisoners in the past decade, prisoners are still less than one-fifth of the convict population, and the vast majority of offenders remain in the community amongst us. If we are to effectively control crime—as opposed to exacting retribution and justice—we must focus our efforts on where the offenders are, which is in the community reporting to probation and parole officers.

Despite the fact that both crime bills were touted by their proponents as comprehensive approaches to the crime problem, neither the 1994 Crime Act nor the 1995 "Taking Back Our Streets" proposal even mentions probation or parole, much less provides funding or direction for revising programs or practices. Moreover, the Federal bill will likely take money away from community corrections budgets, which are already at a dangerously low level, to fund the expanded prison space required to comply with the Federal mandate requiring State prisoners to serve 85 percent of their sentences (the so-called "truth in sentencing" provision).

This policy brief addresses the public safety consequences of current probation and parole practices. It contends that current crime policies are neither comprehensive nor can they be effective unless we focus on the needs and risks posed by probationers and parolees. Whether we are able to control the crime propensities of *these* offenders is critical to the effectiveness of any anti-crime program.

We must rethink the types of programs and funding levels that are appropriate for the kinds of clients these agencies now encounter. The majority of probationers are convicted felons, have prior criminal

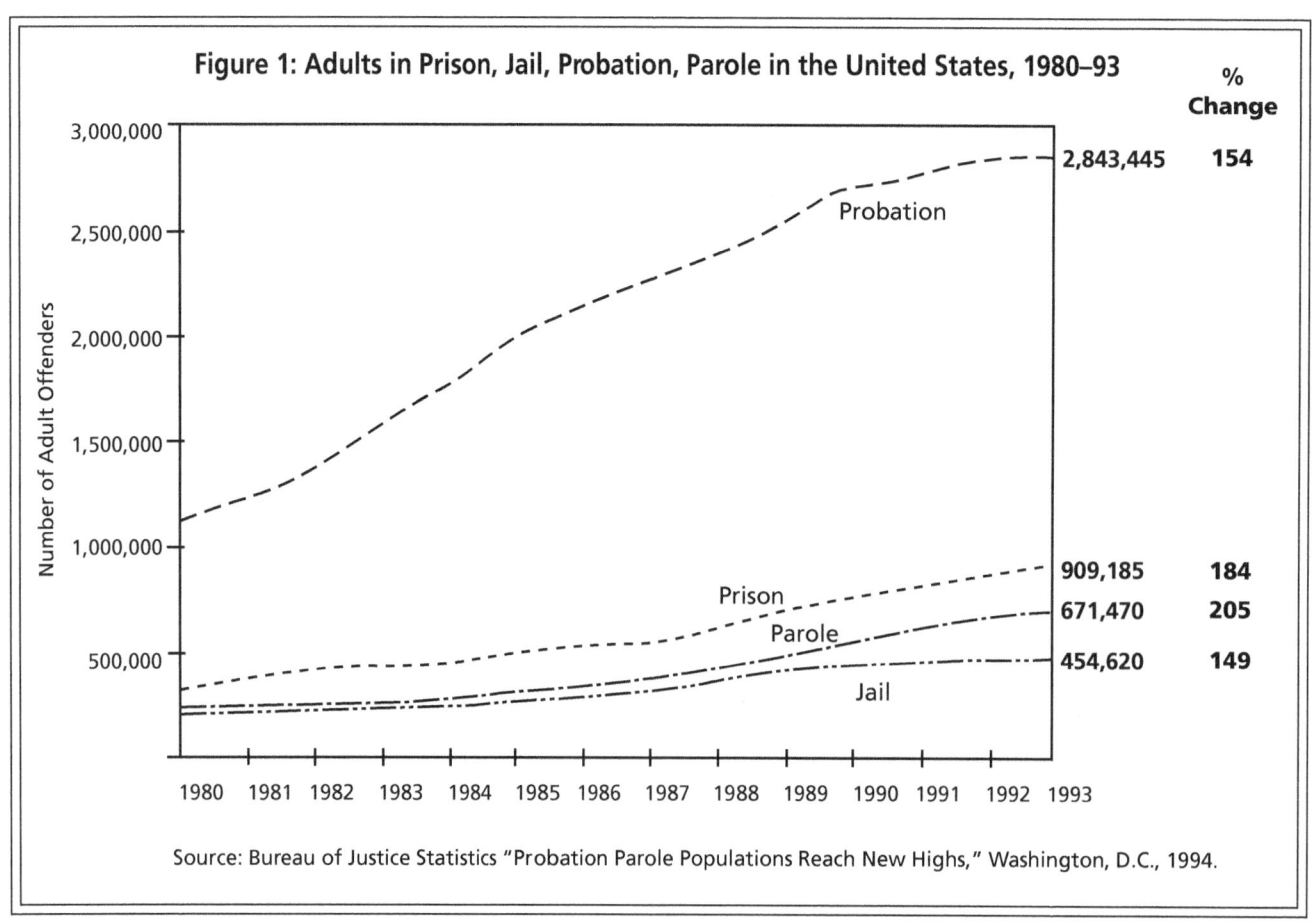

Figure 1: Adults in Prison, Jail, Probation, Parole in the United States, 1980–93

		% Change
Probation	2,843,445	154
Prison	909,185	184
Parole	671,470	205
Jail	454,620	149

Source: Bureau of Justice Statistics "Probation Parole Populations Reach New Highs," Washington, D.C., 1994.

records, and are likely to be substance and alcohol abusers with few marketable skills. If we continue to ignore their behavior—and miss the opportunity to intervene positively—we are relatively assured of imprisoning them eventually. Current policy simply waits until their criminality escalates to the point of needing imprisonment, and such policies have now proven costly and ineffective at reducing crime.

The author suggests developing "surveillance plus treatment" programs for drug-involved probationers, including offenders who are convicted of drug possession and use, but not trafficking. Evaluation research suggests that we now have program models that are effective at reducing their recidivism rates, that the public is supportive of rehabilitation as opposed to incarceration for such offenders, and that the cost-benefit tradeoffs between prison and community corrections are among the highest for that subpopulation.

Who Is On Probation and Parole? A Profile of the Population

There is a huge misunderstanding of the public safety risks and needs posed by offenders currently under community supervision, particularly those on probation. Some might believe that while there are a large number of persons on probation and parole, the public safety risk they pose as a group is minimal. The public often assumes that probation is a sentencing alternative only for misdemeanants or "non-dangerous" offenders.

Many also erroneously assume that as prison populations have grown, those remaining in the community have become increasingly less serious, and hence less in need of supervision. It might seem logical that since prison populations have quadrupled over the past decade, those remaining in the community would be increasingly less serious because the more serious offenders would have been skimmed off and sentenced to prison. Unfortunately, this is not true. As shown in figure 1, populations in all four components of the corrections system have grown at record rates since 1983. And the 3 to 1 ratio of community-based to institutional populations has remained relatively stable for over a decade.

Furthermore, analysis shows that the probation population has become increasingly serious if judged by prior criminal record, current conviction crime, or

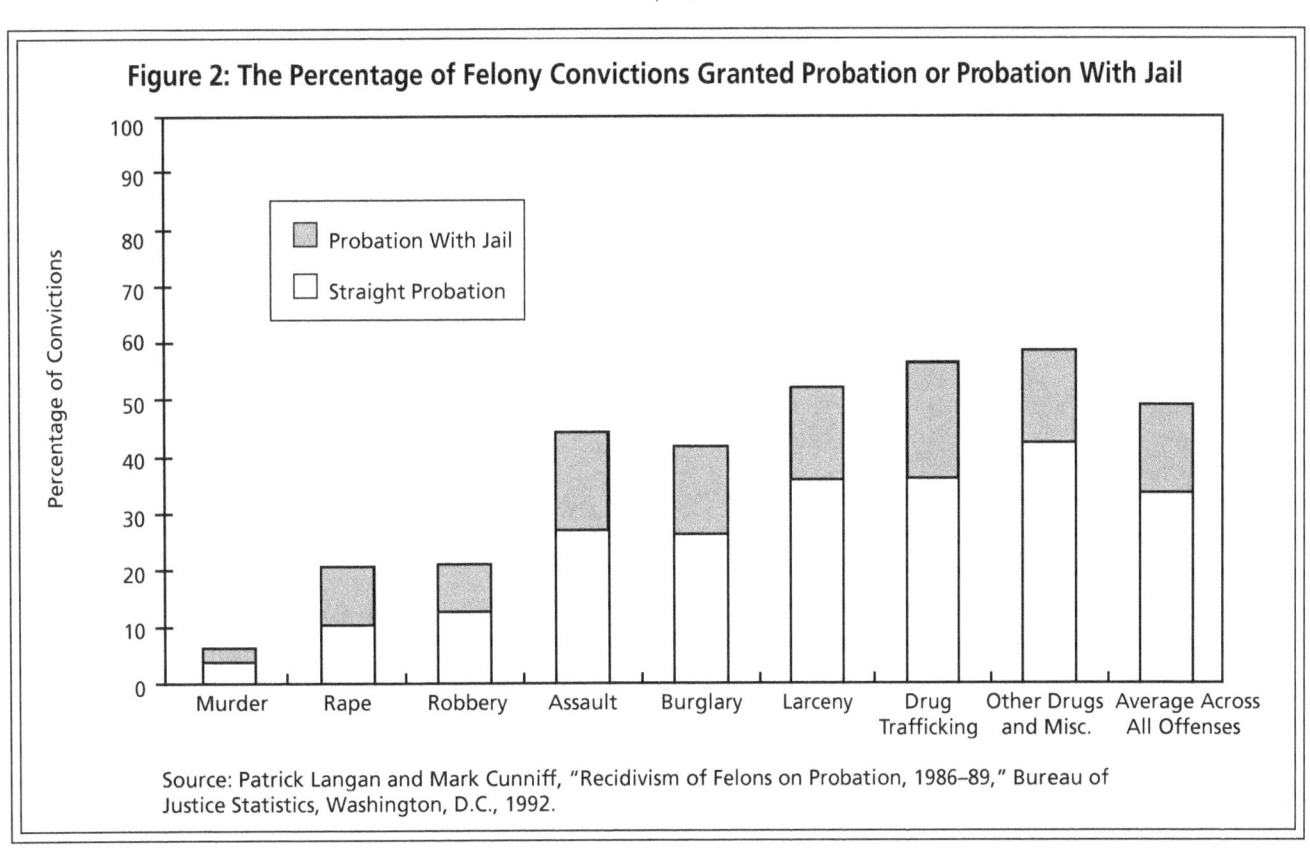

Figure 2: The Percentage of Felony Convictions Granted Probation or Probation With Jail

Source: Patrick Langan and Mark Cunniff, "Recidivism of Felons on Probation, 1986–89," Bureau of Justice Statistics, Washington, D.C., 1992.

substance abuse histories (Petersilia et al., 1985). The truth of the matter is that the overall U.S. population has grown and a greater proportion of U.S. citizens are being convicted, so that all corrections populations have grown in size simultaneously.

The Bureau of Justice Statistics (BJS) tracks sentences handed down by the courts in felony convictions. The agency reports that in 1986 the courts granted probation to 46 percent of all convicted felons (Langan and Cunniff, 1992). As shown in figure 2, about 30 percent of these defendants were also required to serve some jail time. Considering different crime types, about 6 percent of murderers were placed on probation, as were 20 percent of convicted rapists. Twenty percent of convicted robbers and 40 percent of burglars were similarly sentenced to probation rather than to active prison terms. The average sentence to probation was just under 40 months, and an average jail term (where it was imposed) was 6 months.

Table 1 shows the conviction crimes of all adults under correctional supervision during 1991.

Table 1 shows that about 16 percent of probationers were convicted of violent crimes, as were 26 percent of parolees. This means that on any given day in the United States in 1991, there were an estimated 435,000 probationers and 155,000 parolees residing in local communities who had been convicted of violent crime—or over half a million offenders. If we compare that to the number of violent offenders residing in prison during the same year, we see that there were approximately 372,500 offenders convicted of violent crime in prison, and approximately 590,000 outside prison and in the community on probation and parole. Overall, we can conclude that nearly three times as many violent offenders (1.02 million) were residing in the community as were incarcerated in prison (372,500). These numbers make painfully clear why a failure to provide adequate funding for community corrections invariably places the public at risk.

Of course, the type of crime an offender is convicted of does not necessarily equate with his or her risk of recidivism. Patrick Langan at BJS tracked for 3 years a sample representing nearly 80,000 felons granted probation in 1986. Just over 40 percent of the probationers were classified by probation departments as needing either "intensive" or "maximum" supervision—meaning they appeared to be at a high risk of recidivating based on their prior criminal records and need for services. If probationers are growing in numbers and becoming more serious, they are in need of more supervision, not less. But less is exactly what they have gotten over the past decade.

Despite the unprecedented growth in probation populations and their more serious clientele, probation budgets have not grown. From 1977 to 1990, prison, jail, parole, and probation populations all about tripled in size. Yet only spending for prisons and jails had accelerated growth in overall government expenditures. In 1990 prison and

Table 1: Adults Under Correctional Supervision, By Offense, 1991

| Most Serious | Percentage of Adult Offenders | | | |
Offense	Probation	Jail	Prison	Parole
All offenses	100%	100%	100%	100%
Violent offenses	16	22	47	26
Homicide	1	3	12	4
Sexual assault	2	3	9	4
Robbery	2	7	15	11
Assault/other	10	8	10	6
Property offenses	34	30	25	36
Burglary	7	11	12	15
Larceny/theft	16	8	5	12
Auto theft	1	3	2	2
Fraud/other	10	8	6	6
Drug offenses	24	23	21	30
Trafficking	8	12	13	18
Possession/other	16	11	9	2
Public-order offenses	25	23	7	7
Weapons	1	2	2	2
DWI/DUI	16	9	NA	3
Other	9	14	5	3

Sources: Bureau of Justice Statistics initiatives, including Census of Probation and Parole, 1991; Survey of Inmates in Local Jails, 1989; and Survey of Inmates in State Correctional Facilities, 1991.

jail spending accounted for 2 cents of every State and local dollar spent, twice the amount spent in 1977. Spending for probation and parole accounted for two-tenths of 1 cent of every dollar spent in 1990, unchanged from what it was in 1977 (Langan, 1994). Today, although nearly three-fourths of correctional clients are in the community, about one-tenth of the correctional budget goes to supervise them.

The increase in populations, coupled with stagnant or decreasing funding, means that caseloads (the number of offenders an officer is responsible for supervising) keep increasing. Although the 1967 President's Crime Commission recommended that ideal caseloads be about 30 to 1, national averages are now approaching 150 to 1 for probation and 80 to 1 for parole. And in some communities, ratios are much higher. In Los Angeles County, for example, where nearly 70,000 adults are on probation, funding cutbacks have resulted in caseloads reaching several hundred and few direct services. A recent report noted that 60 percent of all Los Angeles probationers are tracked solely by computer and have no contact with an officer (U.S. Advisory Commission, 1993). Texas reports that it has about 400,000 adults on probation, 95 percent of whom are on regular supervision, meaning they are seen once every 3 months.

Nationally, BJS reports that three out of five felony probationers see a probation officer no more than once a month, at best, because actual contacts are often less than the number prescribed. Because of underfunding and large caseloads, probation supervision in many large jurisdictions amounts to simply monitoring for rearrest. As Clear and Braga (1995: 423) recently wrote: "Apparently, community supervision has been seen as a kind of elastic resource that could handle whatever numbers of offenders the system required it to."

But neglect in funding has had serious consequences. As caseloads rise, there is less opportunity for personal contact between officer and offender, limiting any ability of the officer to bring about positive change in the offender, or refer him or her to appropriate community-based resources and programs (which, incidentally, are also being reduced). Court-ordered fines and restitution don't get paid and community service doesn't get performed—all of which further

tarnish probation's image as being too lenient and lacking in credibility.

Robert Kelgord, chief probation officer in Sacramento, California, after reporting that more than half of the probationers he is responsible for go unsupervised, described the overall situation as follows:

> On each judicial day hundreds of California judges sentence thousands of offenders to probation, sternly enumerating the many conditions of probation that are to be enforced by the probation officer. Unfortunately, virtually all of these offenders will never see a probation officer and there will be absolutely no enforcement of the court-ordered conditions. Equally unfortunate is that all of the players in this drama—especially the offender—understand that the offenders will go unsupervised, will have no accountability to the courts, and will, in a high percentage of the cases, simply reoffend (Commission on Future of California Courts, 1993: 159).

Lack of services and supervision undoubtedly contributes to high recidivism rates. It has been continually shown that there is a "highly significant statistical relationship between the extent to which probationers received needed services and the success of probation" (Comptroller General, 1976: 25). As services have dwindled, recidivism rates have climbed. In the national BJS study mentioned earlier, Langan and Cunniff (1992) found that 43 percent of probationers were rearrested for a felony within 3 years of receiving a probationary sentence. The total group of some 79,000 probationers was responsible for nearly 34,000 arrests, including 632 arrests for murder, 474 for rape, and 5,500 for robbery and assaults. By the end of the 3-year period, 26 percent of the probationers had been sent to prison, another 10 percent to jail, and an additional 10 percent were designated absconders with unknown whereabouts. Overall, 46 percent of felony probationers were classified as "failures." It is no wonder—the same study shows that while 53 percent of the sample was characterized as having a drug abuse problem, only 14 percent of the sample participated in any required drug treatment during the 3-year followup period.

Parolees fare no better. BJS statisticians Allen Beck and Bernard Shipley (1989) tracked 108,580 parolees released from prison in 1983. The sample represented more than half of all released State prisoners that year. They found that within 3 years, 62 percent of them had been rearrested for a felony or serious misdemeanor (23 percent for a violent crime), 47 percent were reconvicted, and 42 percent were returned to prison or jail. By the end of 1986, those prisoners who were rearrested averaged an additional 4.8 new charges.

Another means to gauge the contribution of probationers and parolees to the crime problem is to examine the "criminal justice status" of offenders at the time they committed or were arrested for their current crime. Numerous BJS reports provide that information, and the relevant figures are summarized in figure 3. They attest to the contribution of probationers and parolees to the "crime problem," and to the public safety consequences of reducing funding for community corrections. For example, 31 percent of persons on death row in 1992 report committing their murders while under probation or parole supervision. Leaving

such offenders "unattended" is not only bad policy, it leaves many victims in its wake.

The high failure rates of probationers and parolees also contribute significantly to prison crowding. Current estimates show that between 30 and 50 percent of all new prison admissions are community supervision failures. Indeed, offenders who fail under community supervision are the fastest growing component of the prison population.

What Can We Do? A Proposal To Develop an Integrated Treatment/ Control Program for Drug Offenders

The grim situation described above is known to most individuals who work in the justice system or study it. Until we curb the criminal activities of the three-fourths of criminals who reside in the community, real reductions in crime or prison commitments are unlikely. Just as there is growing agreement about the

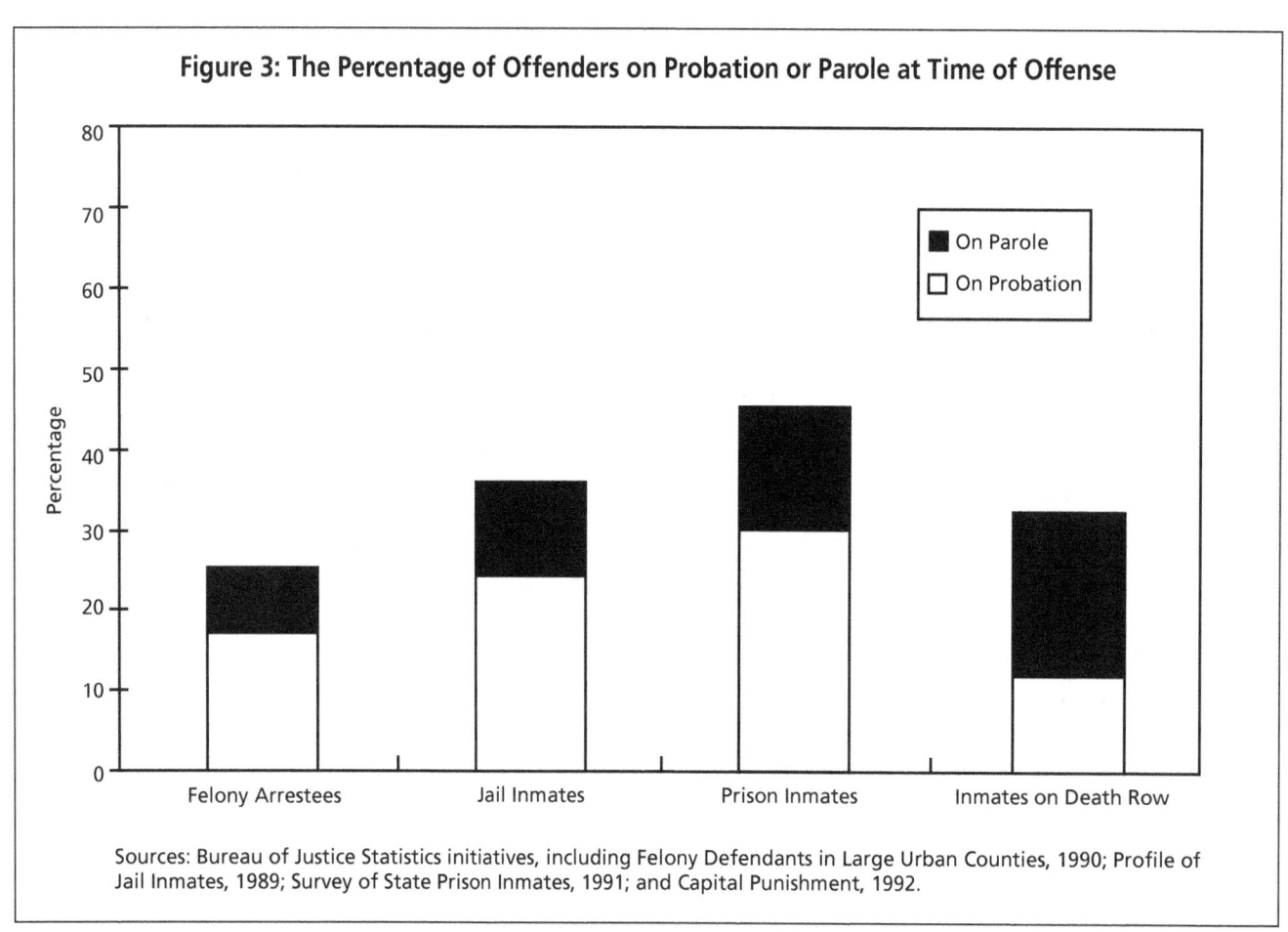

Figure 3: The Percentage of Offenders on Probation or Parole at Time of Offense

Sources: Bureau of Justice Statistics initiatives, including Felony Defendants in Large Urban Counties, 1990; Profile of Jail Inmates, 1989; Survey of State Prison Inmates, 1991; and Capital Punishment, 1992.

nature of the problem, there is also an emerging consensus about how to address it.

We need to first regain the public's trust that probation and parole can be meaningful, credible sanctions. During the past decade, many jurisdictions developed "intermediate sanctions" as a response to prison crowding. These programs (for example, house arrest, electronic monitoring, intensive supervision) were designed to be community-based sanctions that were tougher than regular probation, but less stringent and expensive than prison. The program models were good and could have worked, except for one critical factor: they were usually implemented without creating an organizational capacity to ensure compliance with the court-ordered conditions.

Intermediate sanctions were designed with smaller caseloads, enabling officers to provide both services and monitoring for new criminal activity, but they never were given the resources needed to enforce the sanctions or to provide necessary treatment. When the court ordered offenders to participate in drug treatment, for example, many probation and parole officers could not comply with the request because local treatment programs were unavailable. Similarly, when the court ordered fines or restitution to be paid or community service to be performed, it often was ignored because of a lack of personnel to follow through and monitor such requirements. Over time, what was intended as tougher community corrections in most jurisdictions did not materialize, thereby further tarnishing probation's and parole's image. (For a complete review of this experience, see Petersilia and Turner, 1993; Clear and Braga, 1995.) And while most judges still report being anxious to use tougher, community-based programs as alternatives to routine probation or prison, most are skeptical that the programs promised "on paper" will be actually delivered in practice. As a result, some intermediate sanction programs are beginning to fall into disuse.

But not all programs have had this experience. In a few instances, communities invested in intermediate sanctions and made the necessary treatment and work programs available to offenders. And, most importantly, the programs worked: in programs where offenders received both surveillance (for example, drug tests) and relevant treatment, recidivism was reduced 20 to 30 percent (Petersilia and Turner, 1993). Recent

program evaluations in Texas, Wisconsin, Oregon, and Colorado have found similarly encouraging results (Clear and Braga, 1995). Even in BJS's national probation followup study, it was found that if probationers were participating in or making progress in treatment programs, they were less likely to have a new arrest (38 percent) than either those drug offenders who had made no progress (66 percent) or who were not ordered to be tested or treated (48 percent).

There now exists rather solid empirical evidence that ordering offenders into treatment, and getting them to participate, reduces recidivism. So, the first order of business must be to allocate sufficient resources so that designed programs (incorporating both surveillance and treatment) can be implemented. Sufficient monetary resources are essential to obtaining and sustaining judicial support and achieving program success.

Once we have that in place, we need to create a public climate to support a reinvestment in community corrections. Good community corrections cost money, and we should be honest about that. We currently spend about $200 per year, per probationer for supervision. It is no wonder that recidivism rates are so high. At a minimum, effective treatment programs cost about $12,000 to $14,000 per year. Those resources will be forthcoming only if the public believes that the programs are both effective and punishing.

Public opinion is often cited by officials as the reason for supporting expanded prison policies. According to officials, the public demands a "get tough on crime" policy, which is synonymous with sending more offenders to prison for longer terms. We must publicize recent evidence showing that offenders—whose opinion on such matters is critical for deterrence—judge some intermediate sanctions as *more* punishing than prison. Surveys of offenders in Minnesota, Arizona, New Jersey, Oregon, and Texas reveal that offenders who are asked to equate criminal sentences judge certain types of community punishments as *more* severe than prison.

One of the more striking examples comes from Marion County, Oregon. Selected nonviolent offenders were given the choice of serving a prison term or returning to the community to participate in the Intensive Supervision Probation (ISP) program, which imposed drug testing, mandatory community service, and frequent visits with the probation officer. About a third of the offenders given the option between ISP or prison chose prison. When Minnesota inmates and corrections staff were asked to equate a variety of criminal sentences, they rated 3 years of ISP as equivalent in punitiveness to 1 year in prison (Petersilia and Deschenes, 1994).

What accounts for this seeming aberration? Why should anyone prefer imprisonment to remaining in the community—no matter what the conditions? Some have suggested that prison has lost some of its punitive sting and hence its ability to scare and deter. For one, possessing a prison record is not as stigmatizing as in the past because so many of the offenders' peers (and family members) have also "done time." A recent survey showed that 40 percent of youths in State training schools have parents who have been incarcerated. Further, about a quarter of all U.S. black males will be incarcerated during their lives, so the stigma attached to having a prison record is not as great as it was when it was relatively uncommon. And the pains associated with prison—social isolation, fear of victimization—seem less likely with repeat offenders, who have learned how to do time.

In fact, far from stigmatizing, prison evidently confers status in some neighborhoods. Jerome Skolnick of the University of California, Berkeley, found that for drug dealers in California, imprisonment confers a certain elevated "home boy" status, especially for gang members for whom prison and prison gangs can be an alternative site of loyalty. And, according to the California Youth Authority, inmates steal State-issued prison clothing for the same reason. Wearing it when they return to the community lets everyone know they have done "hard time."

The length of time an offender can be expected to serve in prison has also decreased—latest statistics show that the average U.S. prison term for those released to parole is 17 months. But more to the point, for less serious offenders the expected time served can be much less. In California, for example, more than half of all offenders entering prison in 1995 were expected to serve 6 months or less. Offenders on the street seem to be aware of this, even more so with the extensive media coverage such issues are receiving.

For convicted felons, freedom is preferable, of course, to prison. But the type of program being advocated here—combining heavy doses of surveillance and treatment—does not represent freedom. In fact, as suggested above, such community-based programs may have more punitive bite than prison. Consider a comparison between Contra Costa (California) County's ISP for drug offenders, which was discontinued in 1990 due to a shortage of funds, with what drug offenders would face if imprisoned:

ISP. Offenders are required to serve at least one year on ISP. During ISP, offenders are supervised by probation officers who are responsible for no more than 40 adult offenders. In addition to twice weekly face-to-face contacts, the ISP program included a random drug testing hotline, Saturday home visits, weekly Narcotics Anonymous meetings, special assistance from local police to expedite existing bench warrants, and a liaison with the State Employment Development Department. To remain on ISP, offenders had to be employed or participating in relevant treatment or training, perform community service, pay victim restitution (if required by the court), and remain crime- and drug-free.

or

Prison. A sentence of 12 months actually means that an offender will serve about 6 months. During his term, he is not required to work, nor will he be required to participate in any training or treatment, but may do so if he wishes. Once released, he will probably be placed on routine parole supervision, where he might see his officer once a month.

These results are important to publicize, particularly to policymakers, who say they are imprisoning such a large number of offenders because of the public's desire to get tough on crime. But it is no longer necessary to equate criminal punishment solely with prison. The balance of sanctions between probation and prison can be shifted, and at some level of intensity and length, intermediate punishments can be the more dreaded penalty.

Once the support and organizational capacity are there, we need to target an offender group that makes the most sense, given our current state of knowledge committing any illegal activity (-72 percent), and mean months involved in criminal activity (-80 percent).

Regardless of treatment modality, reduction in crime was substantial and significant (although participants in the social model recovery programs had the biggest reduction). In the California study, the most effective treatment programs cost about $12,000 per year, per client.

In summary, there are several steps to achieving greater crime control over probationers and parolees. First, we must provide adequate financial resources to deliver programs that have been shown to work. Successful programs combine *both* treatment and surveillance, and they are targeted to appropriate offender subgroups. Current evidence suggests that low-level drug offenders are prime candidates for the intermediate sanction programs considered here. We must then garner support, convincing the public that the probation sanction is punitive and convincing the judiciary that offenders will be held accountable for their behavior.

Concluding Remarks

Current Federal efforts to curb crime seek simple, politically correct solutions where simple answers do not exist. There are no silver bullet fixes to the crime problem, nor are there any hopeful signs that lead us to expect a spontaneous decline in the problem in the absence of dramatic policy action. If anything, the indicators point to increases in violent youth crime, a trend that will likely continue unless effective steps toward arresting it are taken.

This policy brief argues that current Federal efforts are misguided and do not focus on preventing the crimes of the next generation or de-escalating the criminal careers of those on probation and parole. Dr. Dean Ornish, the guru of the low-fat road to cardiovascular health, shows a cartoon at the opening of his lectures that has application far beyond the topic of cardiovascular disease. The slide shows a crew of doctors frantically mopping up a floor that continues to be flooded by an overflowing sink. The problem, of course, is that no one has turned off the faucet.

Current crime policy is similarly focused. Short-term strategies have held sway at the expense of long-term prevention programs. We remain so consumed by the overwhelming challenge of providing cells for those imprisoned that we have little energy (or money) to address the more fundamental questions of how to prevent the ever-increasing number of people who choose to enter a life of crime or the continued criminal escalation of probationers and parolees.

Of course we must continue to imprison the violent. It is a false dichotomy to argue between tough law enforcement and community-based crime prevention programs. The choice is not one or the other—it must be both. We need to create enough prison space to incarcerate the truly violent, but we also must support programs to reduce the flood tide of criminals that current conditions create.

It will not be easy, so we had better start now.

References

Beck, Allen and Bernard Shipley, "Recidivism of Prisoners Released in 1983," Bureau of Justice Statistics, Washington, DC, 1989.

Blumstein, Alfred, "Youth, Violence, Guns, and the Illicit-Drug Industry," Heinz School of Public Policy and Management, Carnegie-Mellon University, Working Paper 94–29, 1994.

Clear, Todd and Anthony A. Braga, "Community Corrections," in *Crime*, edited by James Q. Wilson and Joan Petersilia, Institute for Contemporary Studies, San Francisco, California, 1995.

Commission on the Future of the California Courts, *Justice in the Balance, 2020*, Sacramento, California, 1993.

Drug Strategies, *Keeping Score*, Washington, DC, 1995.

Gerstein, Dean, et al., *Evaluating Recovery Services: The California Drug and Alcohol Treatment Assessment (CALDATA)*, Department of Alcohol and Drug Programs, State of California, 1994.

Institute of Medicine, Committee for the Substance Abuse Coverage Study (D.R. Gerstein and H.J.

Harwood, eds.), *Treating Drug Problems*, Vol. 1, "A Study of the Evolution, Effectiveness, and Financing of Public and Private Drug Treatment Systems," National Academy Press, Washington, DC, 1990.

Langan, Patrick and Mark A. Cunniff, "Recidivism of Felons on Probation, 1986-89," Bureau of Justice Statistics, Washington, DC, 1992.

Langan, Patrick, "Between Prison and Probation: Intermediate Sanctions," *Science*, Vol. 264, 1994.

Petersilia, Joan and Elizabeth Piper Deschenes, "Perceptions on Punishment: Inmates and Staff Rank the Severity of Prison versus Intermediate Punishments," *The Prison Journal*, Vol. 74, 1993.

Petersilia, Joan, "Crime and Punishment in California: Full Cells, Empty Pockets, and Questionable Benefits," California Policy Seminar, Berkeley, California, 1993.

Petersilia, Joan, Susan Turner, James Kahan, and Joyce Peterson, *Granting Felons Probation: Public Risks and Alternatives*, RAND, R–3186–NIJ, Santa Monica, California, January 1995.

Schiraldi, Vincent, "Some Gift—For $1.4 Billion, We Pay $31 Billion," *Los Angeles Times,* Opinion Section, B13, March 15, 1995.

Simon, Paul, in New Survey, "Wardens Call for Smarter Sentencing, Alternatives to Incarceration, and Prevention Programs," United States Senate Press Release, Washington, DC, December 21, 1994.

U.S. Advisory Commission on Intergovernmental Relations, *The Role of General Government Elected Officials in Criminal Justice*, Washington, DC, 1993.

Three-Strikes Legislation: Prevalence and Definitions

THREE-STRIKES AND YOU'RE OUT LEGISLATION

Summary

Issues

Efforts to reduce violent crime and deal more effectively with repeat offenders have led to a wide range of legislative initiatives across the Nation. Among the many sentence enhancement options available for dealing with habitual offenders, the three-strikes initiative has found much resonance with the public and legislators alike. Proponents view three-strikes sentencing legislation as the solution for dealing with the persistent, serious, and violent offender. Advocates promise that these types of sentences will both reduce crime and, ultimately, save taxpayers money. This is because they believe that three-strikes would not only decrease the cost of victimization through incapacitation, but would also reduce the not insubstantial costs of re-arrest and reprocessing of repeat offenders by the criminal justice system.

A recent RAND assessment of California's three-strikes legislation points to its potential for reducing serious and violent crime, but at an estimated cost of about $5.5 billion over the next 25 years. A second long-term effect on costs will be the unprecedented growth of the elderly in prisons, which will contribute to higher costs because of their health needs (expected to be double or triple that of inmates from the general population).

Although more research is required on the relationship between age and crime, it is clear that categorical sentencing schemes, such as three-strikes, countervail existing knowledge:

- Statistically speaking, recidivism is known to decline with increases in age.

- Offending at an early age is highly predictive of long criminal careers.

- Attention should be focused on crime prevention and early intervention among youths, before they become ensnared in criminal careers.

- Mandatory sentencing cannot take into account all the circumstances affecting individual cases or their various factual permutations.

Short-term effects of this legislation include a clogged court system causing rising court costs and intolerable delays in civil cases; early release of sentenced felons to make room for three-strikes detainees; and increased discretionary power for prosecutors.

Policy recommendations

- **Impact analysis.** The Attorney General should initiate a careful study of how the Federal three-strikes law is impacting the Federal courts and corrections system. Beyond that, further expansions of the Federal statute should be resisted until the analysis has been completed.

- **Informing the public.** Since the current punitive atmosphere permeates the public and body politic, the public needs to be informed of the true cost and consequences of categorical sentencing schemes. As the Nation's first law enforcement officer, the Attorney General, along with the National Institute of Justice, are in the best position for getting the correct information out to the citizenry objectively and fairly.

- **Criminal justice dialog.** The Attorney General and the National Institute of Justice should consider the development of appropriate mechanisms for beginning a dialog with prosecutors and victim advocates who are fueling the public debate on three-strikes laws. Similar mechanisms are needed to tap the abilities and experiences of judges for developing the kind of sentencing legislation that optimizes discretion to allow consideration of individual differences among offenders, while checking the abuses of the current mandatory systems.

- **Research needs.** The National Institute of Justice should encourage and assist Federal and State legislative bureaus in the development of appropriate research tools and studies to estimate the impact of mandatory sentencing bills, on both costs and crime rates. Legislators and the public must understand the likely impact of such laws, not only in terms of costs and consequences for prison crowding, but also in terms of related processes and issues, such as the negative effects on the civil court system, and the diversion of scarce resources from education, health and welfare, the infrastructure, and other vital public services.

- **Alternative sentencing.** The National Institute of Justice should encourage the development of alternative sentencing policies that may achieve the same crime reduction benefits as three-strikes laws at considerably less cost and assist in their evaluation, in terms of crime reduction and costs. Other "lifetime sanctions," such as intensive supervision, community service, etc., should be pursued. However, research should accompany these programs to document their effect on public safety.

- **Early intervention and prevention.** Given the likelihood that investment in youth crime prevention and early intervention programs may well be more effective than three-strikes legislation, the Attorney General should direct the allocation of Federal funding toward such programs. The collateral benefits of "front-end" investments are likely to consist of improved scholastic and economic performance of those involved in the programs.

- **Regional conferences.** The Attorney General should consider convening a series of regional conferences to explore the findings of existing research on the public safety impact and cost implications of various three-strikes laws. The relative costs and benefits of early childhood crime prevention efforts, early intervention, and alternative sentencing programs should also be examined.

THREE-STRIKES LEGISLATION: PREVALENCE AND DEFINITIONS

Efforts to reduce violent crime and deal more effectively with repeat offenders have led to a wide range of legislative initiatives across the Nation in the past few years. Among the many sentence enhancement options available for dealing with habitual offenders, the three-strikes initiative, first passed in Washington State in 1993, has found much resonance among the general public and legislators alike. By late 1994 no less than 13 States had passed three-strikes sentencing laws.[1] They are California, Colorado, Connecticut, Georgia, Indiana, Kansas, Louisiana, Maryland, New Mexico, North Carolina, Tennessee, Virginia, and Wisconsin. At least eight other States—Alaska, Illinois, Nevada, New Jersey, Ohio, Pennsylvania, South Carolina, and Vermont—have similar legislation pending.

Proponents view three-strikes sentencing legislation as the solution for dealing with the persistent, serious, violent offender—proverbially the three-time loser. Depending on specific formulations, three-strikes laws can be far reaching or narrowly focused. In general, the majority of these provisions call for enhanced penalties for offenders with one or more prior felony convictions. These laws require that offenders serve several years in prison in addition to the penalty imposed for their current offense. The remainder of habitual offender laws are geared to respond to specific types of prior offenses, such as crimes of violence, sex offenses, or crimes perpetrated with guns. Under these types of sentencing provisions, felons found guilty of a third serious crime can be incarcerated for 20 years or more, while offenders convicted of a third violent crime may draw life imprisonment without the possibility of parole.

With few exceptions, three-strikes laws are mandatory, leaving judges no discretion for deviating from the sentences prescribed by the legislatures.[2] Still, the most pronounced characteristic of three-strikes legislation is the extraordinary length of prison terms being imposed. For example, the laws of Georgia, Indiana, Louisiana, Maryland, Tennessee, Washington, and Wisconsin mandate life without the possibility of parole, while offenders serving life sentences in California and North Carolina become eligible for parole only after serving 25 years, in New Mexico after 30 years, and in Colorado after 40 years.[3]

Examples of Three-Strikes and Related Legislation

Legislation passed in Washington and California are prototypical examples of wide-ranging three-strikes laws. For example, under the provisions of Washington's Initiative Measure 593, titled the "Persistent Offender Accountability Act," any person meeting the definition of "persistent offender" must be sentenced to a term of life imprisonment without the possibility of parole.[4] Persistent offenders are defined as persons who have been convicted of a felony considered to be a "most serious offense" in addition to having two prior separate felony convictions. "Most serious offenses" include a wide variety of offenses ranging from murder, assaults, and robbery to burglary, indecent liberties, and promoting prostitution.[5]

California's three-strikes legislation was passed in March 1994 and subsequently ratified by voters in the form of a referendum in the fall of that year. This means that any changes in the law would require a two-thirds vote in the legislature. It surpasses any other legislation on the books in terms of reach and punitiveness. Under its provisions, the first two serious felonies are counted as two strikes. The broad sweep of the law is activated with the commission of "any subsequent felony" or third strike. At this point, a mandatory life sentence is imposed. Three-strikes offenders must spend a minimum of 25 years in prison. In addition, under the new law, sentences are doubled for the second strike, and prisoners must serve their penalty in prison rather than under community supervision or at the local jail. Additionally, "good time" earned in prison is reduced from the previous 50 percent to 20 percent of one's "enhanced" prison term.[6]

Nevada's pending "super habitual offender" legislation narrows the focus somewhat by concentrating on repeat offenders who commit serious felony crimes that are either violent or sex-related.[7] It proposes a super habitual statute that would be triggered by a third violent or sex-related felony and draw a life sentence with or without parole.

Slightly more measured, Vermont's proposed legislation for violent career criminals and habitual criminals focuses on repetitive, violent crime. It sets a mandatory minimum of not less than 15 years for a conviction for a third felony crime of violence, if preceded by two previous violent felony convictions.[8] But judges could still sentence to a maximum term of imprisonment up to and including life. In addition, persons sentenced under the provisions of this legislation would not be eligible for probation, early release, furlough, or parole release until after the minimum prison term has been served.

Additional permutations of three-strikes laws exist in Michigan, where prosecutors have the option of seeking harsher sentences based on prior felony convictions, and in Minnesota, where judges can no longer deviate from existing sentencing guidelines when offenders have been convicted of a third violent crime.

The U.S. Government has entered the three-strikes arena with the passage of the Violent Crime Control and Law Enforcement Act of 1994, better known as the Federal Anti-Crime Act. The legislation provides financial incentives to States in return for increasing their penalties for violent offenders. In essence, the Truth-in-Sentencing Incentive Grants promise Federal moneys based on a formula calculated on the number of violent crimes in each State. However, before receiving the grants, States must change their penal codes so that offenders with a second violent crime would have to serve a minimum of 85 percent of their prison sentence. States would also have to increase the percentage of all violent offenders sentenced to prison, eliminate parole for two-strike violent offenders, and increase the time served by such prisoners.

Effects of Three-Strikes Legislation

The idea of incarcerating repeat offenders for very long prison terms, including life without parole, has certainly caught fire in the public imagination.

Advocates promise that these types of sentence will not only reduce crime but will ultimately save taxpayers money. This is because they believe that three-strikes would not only reduce the cost of victimization through incapacitation but would also reduce the substantial costs of rearrest and reprocessing repeat offenders by the criminal justice system.

The task force has analyzed the early assessments of the effects of three-strikes and related legislation and questions the validity of the assumptions on which it is based.

RAND's Analysis of California's Three-Strikes Law

The first serious attempt to estimate the costs and benefits of California's three-strikes law was recently published by RAND.[9] Researchers constructed an analytic model for estimating crime rates and costs of the ways in which populations of offenders on the street and in prison would change under the provisions of the new three-strikes law. They also tested four alternative sentencing schemes: (1) a two-strikes-only option; (2) a paradigm focusing on violent felons only; (3) a design treating violent offenders more harshly, while treating minor offenders more leniently; and (4) a guaranteed-full-term scheme under which three-strikes provisos are abandoned, and offenders convicted of serious or violent felonies (including those without any prior strikes) must serve their full sentences without the benefit of "good-time" deductions.

The results of RAND's assessment shed considerable light on the sentencing debate. They also provide some interesting and not entirely unexpected findings. For example, there are definite trade-offs among the various schemes. In essence, the more focused sentencing alternatives are less costly than the three-strikes option provided by the current law. But the alternatives are also less effective for reducing crime.

Of the four alternative sentencing schemes tested, the option that reserves extended sentences exclusively for violent felons turns out to be the best possible option in terms of costs and benefits. This is because it delivers two-thirds of the crime reduction of three strikes at half the cost. As it is written, California's three-strikes legislation has the capacity over the next 25 years to reduce the annual number of serious crimes to 28 percent below the number of offenses that would have been committed under the previous law.[10] While this is unquestionably a significant crime reduction, it comes unfortunately with an increase in cost to taxpayers of about $5.5 billion a year over the same time period. The two-strikes option and the scheme that punishes serious offenders more severely while treating minor offenders more leniently, fall between these two options in terms of cost and potential crime reductions.

One of the more interesting RAND findings involves the guaranteed-full-term sentencing scheme. It matches the current three-strikes law in crime reduction, and it does so at less cost. The model also has some added advantages. Because it incapacitates offenders early in their criminal careers by giving short prison terms to first-time serious felons, while three-strikes imposes long sentences to a few at the end of their careers, its incapacitating effects correspond with the well-known relation between age and crime. Criminologically speaking, it makes little sense to invest scarce resources by incarcerating offenders whose prime offending years are behind them.

California's Legislative Analyst's Office Assessment of the State's Three-Strikes Law: A Lesson About Unintended Consequences

The most recent assessment of California's three-strikes law comes from the State's Legislative Analyst's Office (LAO).[11] In essence, it identifies a number of problems associated with the three-strikes legislation and lists a series of unintended consequences. First, rather than concentrate the full weight of the law on the serious, violent offender, a majority (about 70 percent) of defendants charged under three-strikes are nonviolent, standing accused of petty theft and drug possession.

Second, the law has seriously impacted plea bargaining rates. Under the old law, more than 90 percent of all felony cases were concluded through plea bargains. Under three-strikes, this number has dwindled to 14 percent of two-strikes cases, and a mere 6 percent of three-strikes cases. It appears that private de-

fense attorneys and public prosecutors advise their clients that they have little to lose by refusing to plea bargain. Not surprisingly, the State is experiencing large increases in jury trials. For example, Los Angeles County expects its jury trials to more than double. More than 5,000 such trials are expected in the county this year alone. This is bad news for anyone hoping to get a civil case heard in California courts. Criminal cases take precedence under the speedy-trial rules, and the tremendous increase in jury trials has consumed all resources.

Third, three-strikes has adversely affected jails in several ways. LAO found that counties tend to set bail for two-strikes defendants at twice the usual rate, while three-strikes defendants may be refused bail altogether. As a result, already overcrowded jails are crowded further. The cost of jail supervision is higher for this offender population because it is considered to be a higher security risk. Perhaps worst of all, the incarceration of two- and three-strikes detainees is forcing jails to release other inmates early. For example, the time served by inmates in the Los Angeles County jail system has dropped from about two-thirds of their sentence to less than 50 percent, surely an unintended consequence of the new three-strikes law.

Fourth, as has been amply documented in other States with inflexible sentencing laws, prosecutors, judges, juries, and even crime victims find ways to circumvent the intent of the three-strikes legislation in California. This is because they perceive injustice in certain cases and think that the punishment simply does not fit the crime. In such instances, charges will be changed to lesser offenses, and judges can convert prior felony offenses to misdemeanors or even refuse to consider the existence of prior felony records. In that sense, discretion in criminal justice is analogous to the third law of thermodynamics. Like energy, it cannot be eliminated, only displaced.

Fifth, even though California's prison population is growing by 300 to 400 inmates a week, the full impact of three-strikes has yet to be felt by the State prison system. This is because too few cases have reached the point of conviction and sentencing under the new law. Nonetheless, LAO findings confirm RAND's inmate population and cost projections. By 1999, the California Department of Corrections expects its prison population to have increased by roughly 70 percent to a total of 211,000. Given that growth rate, the State will have to build at least another 15 institutions at an estimated cost of several billion dollars.

Sixth, California's crime rates have dropped 6.7 percent during the first half of 1994. That trend appears to be holding. However, whether or not that means three-strikes is working is less clear. This is because the crime rates had begun to decline prior to the passage of this legislation and may be largely independent of it.

Nevada's Analysis of the Super Habitual Offender Statute: The High Cost of Three-Strikes to Small Systems

It will be recalled that Nevada is contemplating the passing of a super habitual offender law that targets offenders convicted of a third violent or sex-related felony. At the legislature's request, Nevada's Legislative Counsel Bureau conducted a limited analysis of the fiscal impact of this legislation based on actual prisoner intake information derived from its prison system.[12] Dealing with a much smaller inmate population than California, the Bureau identified only seven inmates as potential candidates for the super habitual offender law. Three of the seven were already serving more severe sentences than those contemplated under the new law (two are on death row and one is serving two consecutive life sentences). Using 37 years as a life term (based on Nevada's experience), the Bureau determined that the 4 remaining inmates would have to "collectively serve an additional 81 years beyond their current sentences" had the new three-strikes legislation been in effect. The Bureau then multiplied the fiscal year 1993 cost of keeping one inmate ($14,188) by 81. This yields a total of $1,149,228 in additional costs to the system for four inmates, directly attributable to three-strikes legislation. The Bureau purposefully did not include the added costs of inflation, increases in the crime rate, or rising capital, administrative, and operations costs in its calculations. Had they done so, the total cost would have been significantly higher.

Texas' Assessment of Federal Truth-in-Sentencing Grants

In January 1995, the Criminal Justice Policy Council of Texas assessed the potential impact of the recent Federal anti-crime initiatives.[13] Its report concludes that "if Texas abolishes parole for all violent offenders without adopting sentencing guidelines and requires these offenders to serve 85 percent of their sentence, and present sentencing patterns remain the same," the State would need about 10,400 additional prison beds between 1996 and 2000 to accommodate the effects of this policy. Further, even if Texas were to receive all possible Federal moneys allocated to the State under the grant provisions, the funding would not cover the costs of constructing the new prison cells, nor would there be any Federal resources for operational costs. Looking at the the long-term impact of this Federal initiative, the Council estimated that it would generate the need for an additional 50,400 prison beds between 2000 and 2046.[14]

Short-Term Effects of Three-Strikes Legislation on the Criminal Justice System

Based on what is known about the experiences with three-strikes so far, it is clear that this kind of legislation has begun to clog the court system to the choking point. This is due to greatly reduced plea bargaining rates engendered by this type of law. As more and more defendants opt for trials, court capacities will diminish and court costs will rise. To free crowded court calendars, civil cases will be pushed back beyond the point of tolerance of citizens seeking justice. The dramatic changes in plea bargaining are no surprise. Various mandatory sentences have long been on the books across the Nation. For example, New York's tough drug control laws or Massachusetts' gun control legislation prescribe mandatory incarceration of violators. Evaluations of the impact of this type of legislation have shown invariably that it tends to be subverted by practitioners whenever they perceive that injustice would result: "Prosecutors refuse to press for conviction, juries refuse to convict, and judges refuse to sentence people under these provisions. Hundreds of imaginative ways are found at every level of the criminal justice system (including the police) to circumvent the intent of such laws."[15]

Jails, already overcrowded, are being stretched beyond capacity. To make room for three-strikes detainees whose bail is denied for security reasons, more and more sentenced prisoners will have to be released after serving only fractions of their jail terms. And if more dangerous felons are released to make room for the three-strikes detainees, the outcome is certainly less justice, not more.

For those who advocate three-strikes to improve equity in criminal justice, there is little evidence to support their hopes. Studies point to continued racial disparity under enhanced sentencing structures. For example, assessments of related sentencing (such as mandatory prison terms) indicate that legislative efforts to curtail judicial discretion tend to be checkmated by discretion practiced in the prosecutor's office. At that level it is much less open to public scrutiny, where a variety of factors, mostly unrelated to public safety, come into play. Among those factors affecting case processing and outcome are race, pretrial release as opposed to pretrial detention, and the quality and type of defense counsel.[16] As long as prosecutors retain practical control over plea agreements, discretion will be exercised and legislative intent thwarted.

Delayed Effects of Three-Strikes Legislation on Prisons

One of the more insidious effects of three-strikes and related legislation is that the burden of its impact will increase only gradually. In fact, the full weight of these sentence enhancers will not be felt for many years. This delayed impact is because most serious, violent offenders already pull comparatively long sentences while the impact of three-strikes will simply lengthen the time inmates must serve. In the Nevada example, the super sentence would come into effect after 12 years, the time inmates must currently serve. Thus the full fiscal impact of this legislation will not be felt until well into the next century (2033).[17] In South Carolina, the Office of State Budget estimates that the currently contemplated three-strikes law would cost the State $1 billion over the next 14 years with most of the money ($664 million) going toward

prison construction. Here too, inmates and costs could grow incrementally from an additional 157 inmates and $1.9 million in 1996, to 3,273 inmates and $41.1 million in 1999, to a staggering 20,005 new inmates and an additional $251.5 million in 2010.[18] A second, equally slow-growing, long-term effect of three-strikes legislation is the gradual accumulation of elderly inmates in the Nation's prison systems. Even though the percentage of elderly arrested (compared with other segments of the population) is declining, the actual number of elderly who run afoul of the law and are subsequently arrested is increasing in the Nation. Recent counts of older inmates reflect substantial increases in both their number and their percentage in the total population. In fact, prisoners aged 55 years and above more than doubled from 1981 to 1991.[19]

While differences in definitions and incarceration practices make comparisons between States difficult, record numbers of inmates are serving life sentences. In 1990, 11,227 inmates were serving natural life sentences in 30 prison systems.[20] This figure has increased substantially since that time. As of 1994, 17,281 inmates were serving natural life sentences in 36 systems. This represents a 46-percent increase in that offender population.[21] The number of inmates serving 20 years or more has increased from 96,921 in 45 systems in 1990 to 141,026 in 49 systems in 1994, reflecting a 49-percent increase. Such data virtually guarantee that a sizable proportion of any given prisoner population will be growing old and gray in the Nation's State and Federal prison systems.[22]

The unprecedented increase of the elderly in prisons will contribute significantly to the rapid acceleration of the costs of imprisonment because the incidence of health problems is higher among elderly inmates compared with the health needs of elderly in the general population. In general, older inmates tend to have more chronic health problems requiring specialized, continuous health care, including pharmacy services, physical therapy, dietary provisions, skilled nursing care, and related services. About one-third of older offenders are known to experience one or more chronic health problems.[23] These illnesses run the gamut from vision and hearing loss, gastrointestinal disorders, and arthritis to respiratory and cardiovascular problems, cancer, AIDS, tuberculosis, and Alzheimer's disease. The best available estimates for the cost of health care for this elderly inmate population range from double to triple the cost of incarcerating inmates in the general population. This means that prisons must spend on average between $40,000 and $60,000 annually for each seriously chronically ill, older inmate. Because most of them do not represent any serious threat to public safety, the cost of their incarceration adds literally millions of dollars in expenditures with little to show for the investment.

Summary Findings

In summation, the most important consequences of three-strikes, two-strikes, truth-in-sentencing, and related schemes are seen in the fact that each subsequent year will add to the already increasing prison population wherever they are implemented. There will also be huge increases in the cost of incarceration, modified only by fluctuations in the crime rate and the number of offenders qualifying for the enhanced sentences. However, the full fiscal impact of this legislation, akin to Pandora's box, will not unfold until well into the first quarter of the next century, and a prolific source of fiscal troubles it will bring indeed.

The cornerstone of three-strikes and related legislation rests on the twin promises of crime and cost reduction. The previously discussed RAND assessment of California's penal law does point to its potential for reducing serious and violent crime, but at a stunning cost. And while it is too early to attribute with any confidence California's declining crime rate to the new law, there is an unquestionable acceleration in the growth of prisoners and costs, not only in this State but in any other jurisdiction with mandatory sentence enhancement schemes.

The potential of three-strikes and related laws for crime reduction can also be productively assessed by looking at the plethora of criminological research on the relationship between age and crime. In general, crime rates peak during the teenage years. It is axiomatic that crime is a young man's game because most serious crimes are committed by young males between the ages of 14 and 24. After those active years, there is first a rapid decline in criminal activities followed by a gradually diminishing crime rate. The sharp drop in crime rates is seen in the fact that a majority (about 67 percent) of those arrested for violent crime are under 30 years old. However, the true

relationship between age and crime does not quite trace the widely documented age-crime curve because calculations of the average lengths of criminal careers for those arrested for Index crimes show them to be 5.6 years, with residual career lengths peaking between the ages of 30 and 40.[24] These two findings are significant for penal policy development. This is because the greatest potential for incapacitation through incarceration may well be for offenders between the ages of 30 and 40, and not, as is often suggested, for those age 30 and under.[25]

Although more research is required on the relationship between age and crime and the complexities of criminal careers (such as residual career length and incidence), it is clear that categorical sentencing schemes, such as three-strikes and other mandatory options, countervail existing knowledge as follows:

- First, statistically speaking, recidivism is known to decline with increase in age. Hence, long-term incarceration of offenders who will grow old in prison invests scarce resources where they will do the least good if the goal is to reduce recidivism.

- Second, since offending at an early age is highly predictive of long criminal careers, the strongest message of the age-crime curve for policy development lies in focusing attention on crime prevention. Among the firmly established facts in criminological research is that the younger a teen is when first arrested for any criminal behavior, the more likely the youth is to continue in that activity. Therefore, legislatures interested in crime reduction could reap the greatest returns for public dollars by investing them at the front end of the system. The focus should be on the development of a wide range of crime prevention and early intervention programs for youngsters before they become ensnared in criminal careers. Many of these program activites should be outside the criminal justice system and should concentrate on child development, family, and schools.

- Third, mandatory (and related) sentencing schemes appear to be the antithesis of principles of individualization and fairness in criminal justice. This is because sentencing legislation cannot possibly take into account all of the circumstances affecting individual cases or the many factual permutations that exist among various cases. Advocates of sentencing reform believed it would improve fairness in criminal justice through uniformity, openness, and the removal of judicial discretion, but experience thus far indicates that these reforms are neither fair nor effective.

Conclusion and Recommendations

The preceding analysis of the Nation's experience with three-strikes and related penal laws points to the vast differences that exist between the manifest or intended consequences of the legislation and the latent or unintended effects it engenders. In other words, the discrepancies between what is "mandated" or "guaranteed" by the language of these laws and the problems encountered on implementation are characteristic of all significant criminal justice legislation, past, present, and future. These discrepancies occur because the criminal justice system is in reality a very complex organism with no clearly defined head, designed to reconcile the often competing demands among its many constituent parts, of which public safety is but one. Other parts include equity, procedural fairness, efficiency, and consistency. Similar to previous experiences with major legislation in the history of this Nation, three-strikes demonstrates the extreme difficulty in predicting just how the combined reactions of prosecutors, judges, defense attorneys, jurors, defendants, parole boards, and corrections officials will affect the outcome when such legislation is promulgated. Consequently, the only way to safeguard against unintended negative consequences is to monitor the implementation of new laws very closely and make whatever changes are required to achieve the desired goals.

In light of the preceding analysis, the task force has developed the following recommendations:

■ The Attorney General should initiate a careful study of the impact of Federal three-strikes law on Federal courts and corrections systems. Beyond that, further expansion of the Federal statute should be resisted until the analysis has been completed.

■ Since the current punitive atmosphere permeates the public and body politic, the public needs to be informed of the true cost and consequences of categorical sentencing schemes. The Attorney

General, as the Nation's first law enforcement officer, along with the National Institute of Justice, are in the best position for disseminating correct information to the public objectively and fairly.

■ The Attorney General and the National Institute of Justice should consider the development of appropriate mechanisms for beginning a dialog with prosecutors and victim advocates who are presently fueling the public debate on three-strikes laws. Similar mechanisms are needed to enlist the abilities and experiences of judges for developing the kind of sentencing legislation that optimizes discretion to allow consideration of individual differences among offenders while checking the abuses of the current mandatory systems.

■ The National Institute of Justice should encourage and assist Federal and State legislative bureaus in the development of appropriate research tools and studies to estimate the impact of mandatory sentencing bills on both costs and crime rates. At present, analytic techniques and data bases exist for making rough estimates of the impact of any mandatory sentencing law. Both techniques and data bases require refinement. Legislators and the public must understand the likely impact of such laws, not only in terms of costs and consequences for prison crowding, but also in terms of related processes and issues. Among these are the negative effects on the civil court system, and, because public moneys are limited, the diversion of scarce resources from education, health, welfare, the infrastructure, and other vital public services.

■ Because alternative sentencing policies exist that may well achieve the same crime reduction benefits as three-strikes laws at considerably less cost, the National Institute of Justice should encourage their development and assist in their evaluation in terms of crime reduction and costs. Other life-time sanctions such as intensive supervision and community service should be pursued. However, research should accompany these programs to document their effect on public safety.

■ Given the likelihood that investment in youth crime prevention and early intervention programs may well be more effective than three-strikes legislation, the Attorney General should direct the allocation of federal funding toward such programs. The collateral benefits of front-end investments are likely to consist of improved scholastic and economic performance of those involved in the programs.

■ The Attorney General should consider convening a series of regional conferences to explore the findings of existing research on the impact on public safety and cost implications of various three-strikes laws. The relative costs and benefits of early childhood crime prevention efforts and early intervention and alternative sentencing programs should also be examined.

Notes

1. Karpelowitz, A. 1994. "Three Strikes" Sentencing Legislation Update. Denver, CO: National Conference of State Legislatures.

2. Connecticut, Kansas, and Maryland preserve some judicial discretion in their "three strikes" legislation.

3. Karpelowitz, supra note 1.

4. RCW 9.94A.120 and 9.94A.030 (reenacted and amended, January 1993).

5. The Washington State Initiative 593 defines "most serious offenses" as any Class A felony, serious assaults, child molestation, controlled substance homicide, extortion first degree, incest with a child, indecent liberties, kidnapping, leading organized crime, manslaughter, promotion of prostitution, rape, robbery second degree, sexual exploitation, vehicular assault with DUI, any Class B felony with sexual motivation, and any felony with a deadly weapon finding.

6. Greenwood, P.W., C.P. Rydell, A.F. Abrahamse, J.P. Caulkins, J. Chiesa, K.E. Model, and S.P. Klein. (1994). *Three Strikes and You're Out. Estimated Benefits and Costs of California's New Mandatory Sentencing Law.* Santa Monica, CA: RAND.

7. "Criminal Justice System in Nevada." 1994. Legislative Counsel Bureau, Bulletin No. 95–6:13–19. Carson City, NV.

8. Communication from Senator Vincent Illuzzi, Senate Institutions Committee, Vermont Legislative Council, Montpelier, VT, 2–27–95.

9. Greenwood, supra note 6. This section of the discussion is based on the principal findings in the RAND research report.

10. Greenwood, supra note 6, at 18.

11. *The "Three Strikes and You're Out" Law—A Preliminary Assessment.* 1995. Sacramento, CA: Legislative Analyst's Office. This segment of the report is based on the findings of this assessment.

12. Legislative Counsel Bureau, supra note 7, at 15–19. The discussion of this section is based on the findings of the Bureau.

13. Fabelo, T. 1995. Biennial Report to the Governor and the 74th Texas Legislature: The Big Picture Issues in Criminal Justice, Austin, TX:16–18.

14. Fabelo, supra note 13 at 17.

15. Flynn, E.E. May 1976. "Turning Judges into Robots." *The Forensic Quarterly,* V50 N2:143–149.

16. Meierhoeffer, B.S. 1992. "The General Effect of Mandatory Minimum Prison Terms," Washington, DC: Federal Judicial Center; and V. Schiraldi, with M. Godfrey. 1994. "Racial Disparities in the Charging of Los Angeles County's Third 'Strike' Cases." 1994. San Francisco, CA: Center on Juvenile and Criminal Justice.

17. Legislative Counsel Bureau, supra note 7, at 19.

18. *Corrections ALERT,* V l, N23, March 6, 1995.

19. American Correctional Association. 1992. *Directory: Juvenile and adult correctional departments, institutions, agencies and paroling authorities.* Laurel, MD: American Correctional Association; and E.E. Flynn. 1992. "The Graying of America's Prison Population." *The Prison Journal,* V72, N1&2:77–98.

20. Camp, M., and Camp, C.G. 1991. *The corrections yearbook.* South Salem, NY: Criminal Justice Institute.

21. Flynn, E.E. 1995. *Managing Elderly Offenders.* Report to the National Institute of Justice, 93–IJ–CX–0015.

22. Austin, J. (1994). *Three strikes and you're out: The likely consequences on the courts, prisons, and crime in California and Washington State.* San Francisco, CA: National Council on Crime and Delinquency; and M. Camp, and C.G. Camp. 1993. *The corrections yearbook.* South Salem, NY: Criminal Justice Institute; and Tonry, M. 1994. "Drug policies increasing racial disparities in U.S. prisons." *Overcrowded Times,* V5, l:11–14.

23. Anno, B.J. 1990. "The cost of correctional health care: Results of a national survey." *Journal of Prison and Jail Health,* V9 N2:105–134.

24. Blumstein, A., J. Cohen, and P. Hsieh. 1982. *The Duration of Adult Criminal Careers.* Final Report to the National Institute of Justice. Washington, DC: National Institute of Justice. For an excellent discussion of the relationship between age and crime see D.P. Farrington. 1986. "Age and Crime," in *Crime and Justice Review of Research,* M. Tonry and N. Morris, eds., Chicago, IL: The University of Chicago Press, l89–250.

25. Farrington, supra note 18 at 223.

American Crime
Problems From
a Global
Perspective

AMERICAN CRIME PROBLEMS FROM A GLOBAL PERSPECTIVE

Summary

Issues

Transnational crime (i.e., crime violating the laws of several international sovereignties or impacting another sovereignty) has grown incrementally over the past two decades, at a rate roughly corresponding to the increase shown in international trade import-export figures and developments in transportation and communications. Several events demonstrate the stark reality of transnational crimes: the destruction by a terrorist bomb of Pan American Flight 103 over Lockerbie, Scotland, in 1988; the 1993 terrorist bombing of the World Trade Center; the more recent conspiracy in New York City to destroy all Hudson River crossings and both FBI and United Nations headquarters; and the Bank of Credit and Commerce International (BCCI) scam, with an estimated cost to U.S. taxpayers of between $200 billion and $1.4 trillion by the year 2021.

In each of these cases, U.S. law enforcement authorities responded vigorously, but with limited overall success. Our system has been developed to deal with criminality at the city/county level and, in some cases, at the national level. With respect to global crime, however, we lack readiness—in terms of education, research sponsorship, interagency cooperation (between the Departments of Justice and State), and a full commitment to a centralized and coordinated international effort.

Crime is not a strictly local, or even national, problem; although its impact is felt at the local level, much crime is internationally conditioned and coordinated. For instance, the connection between street crime and the importation and dissemination of drugs is well established. Similarly, an increase in fraud crimes is commensurate with growth in the operational reach of commercial transactions. Profits from the international drug trade, "laundered" overseas and reinvested in American real estate, commercial, or entertainment enterprises, significantly affect U.S. citizens, who must pick up the burden for uncollected taxes on these transactions.

In addition, the impact of ethnic gang criminality on our "local" crime scene is readily apparent, e.g., the wholesale trade in cocaine, controlled by illegal immigrants from Colombia; the importation of Chinese slave labor into the U.S. and exploitation of Chinese-American businesses by Chinese gangs (triad-based); trade in arms and drugs by Jamaican gangs; burglaries by Albanian gangs; and involvement in the fuel distribution market and the international trade of weapons and nuclear materials by Russian gangs. These new ethnic gangs maintain intra-ethnic contacts, as well as relations with their countries of origin, and local law enforcement professionals are powerless to stop or control them.

Policy recommendations

- **U.N. Convention.** Section 32098 of the 1994 Crime Act (dealing with the development of a United Nations Convention on Organized Crime) should be retained and further implemented.

- **Overseas deployment.** The achievements of the Federal Government in dealing with the complex problems of transnational crime, including deployment of U.S. law enforcement personnel in overseas stations, should be publicly highlighted and strengthened.

- **Training.** Strategies to deal with transnational crime should require that schools of criminal justice provide more focused training in areas such as geography, geopolitics, foreign criminal justice systems, comparative criminological methods, and global approaches to crime control.

- **Data bases and strategies.** The capacity of the Bureau of Justice Statistics and the National Institute of Justice to develop international data bases and strategies for dealing with transnational crime, in collaboration with the U.N. Crime Prevention and Criminal Justice Branch and groups of American scholars, should be strengthened.

- **Interagency cooperation.** The Departments of Justice and State should strengthen their cooperative efforts to deal with organized crime.

- **Counter-terrorism.** The Omnibus Counter-Terrorism Act of 1995 deserves vigorous implementation and constant evaluation/monitoring of its impact.

- **Global perspective.** Every effort should be made to move the crime control debate out of the current gridlock of national versus local approaches; most local crime is the result of worldwide developments and, thus, falls under the foreign policy clause of the U.S. Constitution.

- **Local perspective.** The effort to deal with "local" crime as the product of worldwide events should focus on criminality pertaining to drugs, fraud, and ethnic gangs—with constant vigilance toward other existing and emerging forms of internationally conditioned criminality.

- **Ethnic recruitment.** To deal with ethnic gang criminality, a vigorous recruitment drive should be initiated to enlist candidates from "new" ethnic minorities who can understand or infiltrate such gangs in affected communities; this recruitment could be part of the community policing program initiative to deploy 100,000 new police officers, or it could be part of the block grant program.

AMERICAN CRIME PROBLEMS FROM A GLOBAL PERSPECTIVE

[I]nternational criminal activity has increased dramatically over the past decade and has been facilitated by modern developments in transportation and communications, relaxed travel restrictions, and the greatly increased volume of international trade....[1]

The American scholarly community in criminology and criminal justice fully supports this congressional finding. It rests solidly on research conducted in this country and abroad. The finding has two major implications. First, it requires national leadership in a global approach to deal with transnational crime. Second, it requires us to rethink "local crime" as no longer being truly locally conditioned but, rather, as being the product of events worldwide. These two issues are taken up in order.

National Leadership in a Global Approach To Deal With Transnational Crime

Transnational crime (crime violating the laws of several international sovereignties or crime with impact in another sovereignty) has grown incrementally over the past two decades, roughly corresponding with the increase in international trade (import-export figures), transportation, and communications. Its reality was brought home starkly with several recent events, of which three may serve to demonstrate the point:

■ The destruction by a terrorist bomb of Pan Am Flight 103 over Lockerbie, Scotland, with the loss of 270 (mostly American) lives, in 1988.

■ The terrorist bombing of the World Trade Center (1993) and the more recent conspiracy to destroy all New York City Hudson River crossings, the New York Federal Bureau of Investigation headquarters, and the United Nations headquarters.

■ The Bank of Credit and Commerce International (BCCI) scam that, it is estimated, will cost U.S.

taxpayers between $200 billion and $1.4 trillion by the year 2021.

In all these cases, U.S. law enforcement authorities have responded vigorously, yet with limited success. Our system has been perfected to deal with criminality at the city and county levels, and with regard to some forms of criminality, at the national level. We are not yet quite ready to deal with global criminality. This lack of readiness can be perceived as follows:

■ At the educational level, our schools of criminal justice have ignored globalization until the early 1990's. Only since then have the textbooks of the field provided global coverage of crime and crime prevention.

■ At the research level, interest in the global approach has been building up only recently. While a substantial body of research and information (especially world crime and justice statistics) is now in existence, an achievement in which the Bureau of Justice Statistics has played a vital role, there are few sponsors for badly needed research.

■ At the operational level, the Administration deserves praise for having perfected a network of U.S. criminal justice personnel serving on overseas assignments, in collaboration with the enforcement agencies of other governments. (In fact, the Administration has not taken enough credit for building up this international outreach. An appropriate information exercise could provide considerable assurance to the American public.)

■ At the interagency level (especially between the U.S. Departments of Justice and State), American researchers have the uneasy feeling that a proper modus operandi has not yet been achieved.

■ At the international level, American researchers are well aware of the difficulties of persuading a relatively isolationist U.S. Senate that full cooperation with international agencies (especially the United

Nations Crime Prevention and Criminal Justice Branch and its institutes, with United Nations peacekeeping missions and participation in regional operations) is in the best national interest of the United States (or the global community of which developments have made us an integral part). But here, too, the Administration deserves credit for actions that have not been brought to the attention of the public in an appropriate manner. We are referring here particularly to Section 320908 of the 1994 Crime Bill:

SEC. 320908. SENSE OF THE SENATE REGARDING THE ROLE OF THE UNITED NATIONS IN INTERNATIONAL ORGANIZED CRIME CONTROL.

It is the sense of the Senate that—

(1) the United States should encourage the development of a United Nations Convention on Organized Crime; and

(2) the United Nations should—

   (A) provide significant additional resources to the Commission on Crime Prevention and Criminal Justice;

   (B) consider an expansion of the Commission's role and authority; and

   (C) seek a cohesive approach to the international organized crime problem.

The Administration deserves credit as well for having followed up on the "Sense of the Senate," by taking a lead role in the 1994 United Nations organized crime conference in Naples, through the presence of the Attorney General, and by signing a Memorandum of Understanding between the National Institute of Justice and the United Nations Crime Prevention and Criminal Justice Branch. Yet far more deserves to be done in this regard. Inasmuch as the world's transnational crime problem can be dealt with only by a centralized, coordinated effort (resting, for want of any other situs, in the United Nations), the United States should follow the example of other nations (Canada, Italy, and Japan, for example) in providing budgetary assistance.

Finally, the Administration should be commended for supporting the Omnibus Counter-Terrorism Act of 1995 that researchers view as a significantly powerful strategy to deal with international terrorists subject to U.S. jurisdiction.

Local Crime—The Product of Worldwide Events Over Which We Have Little Control: A New Challenge

The February 1995 House hearings on the 1995 crime bills centered on the question of whether the Federal Government or local governments are best equipped to deal with the problem of local crime. The conservative view was premised on a concept of crime as being locally conditioned and consequently capable of being dealt with by local authorities. The Administration's view, in contrast, posited crime as a national problem (varying by localities) for which no one locality has the technical competence to develop intervention strategies; rather, it asserted that a reservoir of intervention strategies can be assembled cost beneficially only at the national level.

This latter view would comport with scientific findings. Just as costly cancer or AIDS research can be conducted at only a few highly specialized research hospitals (even then requiring national coordination), so costly crime control research leading to the development of intervention strategies must be centralized.

But even that recognition falls short of the mark, inasmuch as crime is no longer a local or a national problem. Even local crime is now an international problem. Its control, thus, may well fall more clearly under the foreign policy power of the U.S. Constitution (Article II, Section 2.3). This point will be demonstrated by the examples of drug, fraud, and gang criminality.

Drug criminality. The connection between street crime and the importation and dissemination of narcotic drugs is well established. The national Drug Use Forecasting program found that in 1992 between one-half and three-quarters of arrestees had used drugs. This is not the place to reiterate the immense human and financial cost to the Nation (including the cost of incarceration, treatment, quality of life, unemployability, etc.) that the international narcotics trade inflicts on the United States and, by now, Europe and much of the remaining world.

Drugs are predominantly produced overseas; they are traded worldwide, but their impact on the crime rate is local or, cumulatively speaking, national. The components for a global strategy to deal with this global, yet local, crime-inducing phenomenon exist, but have not yet been put into place. U.S. participation in the worldwide efforts of the United Nations Narcotic Drug Programmes has been minimal. Greater national leadership in the development of a global drug control policy is urgently needed, or else local crime of every description cannot be expected to show significant decreases.

Fraud criminality. When banks and other businesses operated on a local level, commercial fraud was a local crime. As our example of the BCCI scandal demonstrates, fraud criminality has become entirely global, so that county-level law enforcement agencies are powerless to combat it. It must not be assumed that the BCCI case is unique. It may be noteworthy for its sheer size, but it is simply demonstrative of the fact that frauds increase incrementally with an increase in the operational reach of commercial transactions. Many, but by no means all, of these are spawned by the international drug trade, the profits of which are laundered overseas and reinvested (in this country or abroad) in anything international fraud cartels (or individuals) deem worthy of investment, ranging from real estate to commercial or entertainment enterprises.

The Administration deserves credit for its active participation in the work of the Financial Action Task Force (FATF) of the leading industrial nations. Perhaps if more were known about such international crime prevention cooperation, that itself would serve as a deterrent.

However, international fraud significantly impacts the quality of life in the United States. Uncollected taxes on vast international (ultimately national) transactions are a burden on legitimate taxpayers. Enterprises in the hands of organized crime are not operated for the common good. It may not be too audacious to ask whether those amassing enormous wealth through international commercial fraud will ultimately control parts of our Government—including the legislative branch.

Gang criminality. Ethnic strife and the drive for ethnic empowerment dominate the international political scene—in Chechnya, Bosnia-Herzegovina and Croatia, the Near East, Somalia, Rwanda and Burundi, the Philippines, Laos, Liberia, and Sierra Leone—not to mention the ethnic conflicts in which immigrant minorities in Europe are the victims. Increasingly, our foreign policy has been drawn into such conflicts, and we are likely to see more of them.

Yet, increasingly and significantly, ethnic problems have also impacted our local crime scene. Thus, the cocaine wholesale trade is controlled by illegal immigrants from Colombia; Chinese gangs (triad-based) control the import of Chinese slave labor, by the hundreds of thousands, into the United States, besides exploiting Chinese-American business enterprises; ruthless Jamaican gangs specialize in the arms and drug trades; Russian gangs—as ferocious as the Mafia—are invading the fuel distribution market and the international trade in weapons, nuclear material, and anything else of value; and Albanian gangs have become experts in burglary. The list could be continued ad infinitum. Our point is that, while vigorous Federal law enforcement has made great progress in dealing with Italian-American organized crime, we have no capacity as yet to deal with the new ethnic organized crime wave that significantly impacts life at the local level.

The new ethnic gangs are maintaining intra-ethnic contacts, as well as relations with their countries of origin. Thus, while the impact is local, the solution must be found at the national and international levels. (Part of the problem is that we have no capacity to understand, let alone infiltrate, the new ethnic gangs. As part of the program to employ 100,000 additional [community police] officers, a recruitment drive to enlist young men and women from diverse "new" ethnic communities into our law enforcement agencies would be in order.)

In sum, much of so-called local crime is the result of international developments over which local law enforcement officials have little, if any, control. In fact, very little crime may be left for a category called purely local. The implications for national leadership and initiative taking in collaboration with the world community are evident.

The Capacity of the Research Community To Assist National Law Enforcement With Respect to Transnational and Internationally Conditioned Local Criminality

Over the past 30 years, starting from modest beginnings, American scholars and researchers of criminology and criminal justice have made vast progress in researching, understanding, and targeting for solution many forms of transnational and internationally conditioned local criminality. The body of research can be found in several thousand books, articles, and research reports. Much of this work has been accomplished without significant assistance from government agencies. Nevertheless, the world has acknowledged the American lead in criminological theory building and the modeling of crime control strategies. We are in the process of losing this lead, as foreign governments and foundations, convinced of their national interest in international crime control, are increasingly strengthening their national capacity (at the governmental and nongovernmental levels) by investment in research and development. It would be wise for the Federal Government to utilize the existing reservoir of skill and talent in cross-national criminological research to modestly invest in this capacity and to harness it in the national interest. We are not calling for a "Manhattan Project" to deal with international criminality as it impacts local crime and thus the quality of life in America. (Actually, why don't we?) Rather, we are looking for leadership that would enable us, in collaboration with our colleagues abroad, and particularly in support of the United Nations global effort, to control international criminality, the font of local crime.

Summary Recommendations

■ Section 320908 of the 1994 Crime Act should be retained and implemented further, especially as outlined herein.

■ The achievements of the Federal Government in dealing with the complex problems of transnational crime should be publicly highlighted.

■ Strategies to deal with transnational crime require a more focused training of young men and women at the Nation's schools of criminal justice in issues including geography, geopolitics, foreign criminal justice systems, comparative criminological methods, and options of global approaches to crime control.

■ The capacity of the Bureau of Justice Statistics and the National Institute of Justice to develop international data bases and strategies for dealing with transnational crime, in collaboration with the United Nations Crime Prevention and Criminal Justice Branch, as well as groups of American scholars, should be strengthened.

■ The successes of the Federal Government in dealing with transnational crime through deployment of U.S. law enforcement personnel in overseas stations should be highlighted and strengthened.

■ Interagency cooperation in dealing with transnational crime must be strengthened.

■ The Omnibus Counter-Terrorism Act of 1995 deserves vigorous implementation and constant evaluation and monitoring as to its impact.

■ Every effort should be made to move the crime control debate out of the current lockjaw of national versus local approaches, because most local crime is the result of worldwide developments falling under the foreign policy clause of the U.S. Constitution.

■ The focal points of the effort to deal with transnational and local crime as the product of worldwide events should be drug, fraud, and gang criminality, with constant vigilance toward other and emerging additional forms of internationally conditioned criminality.

■ To deal with the new ethnic gang criminality as part of the program to deploy 100,000 new police officers (community policing) or as part of the block grant program, a vigorous recruitment drive should be initiated to recruit for affected communities candidates from new ethnic minorities.

Note

1. From the Appendix to Section 320908, in which the House recedes to Section 5106 of the 1994 Crime Bill; this excerpt is nonbinding, bipartisan "report language."

www.ingramcontent.com/pod-product-compliance
Lightning Source LLC
Chambersburg PA
CBHW080255180526
45167CB00006B/2535

* 9 7 8 1 4 9 9 6 2 0 9 6 2 *